Merlin
IN HIS OWN WORDS

CLOSE HAND PRESS
Portland, Oregon

Merlin

IN HIS OWN WORDS

Lessons in Life and Love
from an Old Friend

AS CHANNELED BY

MATAARE

✦

COMPILED AND EDITED BY

GWENDOLYN

Published by Close Hand Press
PO Box 12165
Portland, Oregon 97212-2165
www.closehandpress.com

Mataare, Xiota-Lahmpsa

ISBN: 978-0-9798063-0-8

Book and Cover Design: William Stanton
Editor: Aurelia Navarro
Printing: PrintSync, Portland, Oregon
Printed in the United States of America

Disclaimer Notice: Judgment as to the suitability or applicability of the information herein for the purchaser's purposes is necessarily the purchaser's responsibility. Neither the author nor publisher extends any warranty, makes representations or assumes responsibility as to the accuracy or suitability of such information for the purchaser's intended purposes or for consequences of its use. The material in this book is not intended as expert advice, medical or otherwise. If advice or other expert assistance is required, the services of a competent professional person should be sought. The publisher and author, therefore, specifically disclaim any liability, loss or risk, corporate, organizational or personal or otherwise, which may occur as a consequence, directly or indirectly, of the reading, use or application of any part of the contents of this book, which book is sold with that understanding in mind.

Printing number
9 8 7 6 5 4 3 2 1

*This book is dedicated to those who teach: Gurus, Ascended
Masters, Guides, Teachers all—found in zendos and
ashrams, in the quiet of our hearts, in our families, amongst
our friends, in the faces of strangers, in the mystery of the
Wild and the creatures that inhabit it —companions
on the journey Home.*

✦

LA POESIA

. . . And something ignited in my soul,
fever or unremembered wings,
and I went my own way
deciphering
that burning fire
and I wrote the first bare line,
bare, without substance, pure
foolishness,
pure wisdom
of one who knows nothing,
and suddenly I saw
the heavens
unfastened
and open.

Pablo Neruda
(translated by David Whyte)

CONTENTS

FOREWORD

When I met Mataare, my life—in Spirit and in the world—changed inalterably . "For the better" would be a gross understatement.

I suppose the easiest way to describe that impact is this: I fell in Love. I fell in Love with the Guides. I fell in Love with Mataare. I fell in Love with God, the mountains and the streams, the cities, and the world. I fell in Love with you. And, slowly, slowly, I fell in Love with me.

Love creates awe and gratitude swiftly follows. I was flooded with thankfulness, and that thankfulness needed expression or I knew I would explode. It occurred to me that I could make some manner of book of the magnificent transmissions that came through Mataare. I began to collect tapes of his sessions. Hundreds and hundreds of tapes. I listened to them all, and, whenever I had some extra money, I would have my favorites transcribed.

These tapes were of Spirit Guides speaking of struggle, effort, relationships, entanglements, and the limitations of this sensual body. Those ineffable Light entities spoke of Love, Light, Service, and the Divine. They sent dimensions of their being to us through mediums—in this case, through Mataare—and also through our own connection with the Divine. They didn't have bodies but they did have voices; and those voices were not just audible to the listening ear but deeply resonant with the listening heart.

I met Mataare in 1994, after a friend badgered me to come hear and see "the purest trance-channel on the planet" and the "Guides" who came through him (whatever that meant). I finally showed up on a Saturday afternoon. When I walked in the room, I saw a nicely round man in a soft chair. He looked normal. He was laughing. His laughter sounded like music to me. I was drawn. I sat, Mataare went into trance, and the heavens opened.

Actually, Mataare seemed to disappear as he went into what was obviously an altered state. He closed his eyes, slumped over . . . and moments later *someone* else was there. That was clear even to my uninitiated eyes. Another being sat in that same soft chair, someone with the same arms, legs, face, and clothes as Mataare, but he was definably not Mataare. He was a Guide.

What that Guide's exact name was that first day escapes me now. Over the ensuing months, many came through: Miriam, mother to Yeshuwa; Phylos, Keeper of Akasha; Enoch, writer in Light; Davorra, Queen of the Tarot; Q'uan Yin, Goddess of Compassion; Dr. Usui, creator of the healing form known as Reiki; Dr. Milton Erickson; Dr. Song; Milarepa; Yogananda (who always begins by singing); Isis, the Great Mother; Chief Great White Eagle and SunBear, holder of the SunBear energy over the millennia.

And, of course, Merlin.

I met Merlin early on. I remember thinking that I liked his mind. And he was very amusing, in an English Gentleman sort of way. And smart. Merlin spoke of geometries and mathematics and Love. And even though I am not a scientist by training, I understood him. In that indescribable way by which Spirit communicates, I got his message. And it delighted me.

Later I found out that I was connected to Merlin through several other lifetimes—or so he said. I never experienced that first hand; but Merlin did seem to know me pretty darn well, especially my flaws and quirks, the very ones that had dogged me for decades. But he didn't dwell on these. Mostly he laughed.

Flaws, I learned, were simply part of the mix. We are imperfect beings, perfect only in that imperfection. So we had better learn to enjoy it. I learned that the quest for perfection was in fact an errant notion, particularly dangerous for me. I learned that forgiveness was the antidote.

There was so much forgiveness in the Guides, so much Love—a high Love that rang with mercy, compassion, humor, and kindness. I think it was the kindness that staggered me the most. An unfailing kindness that I slowly realized came from an unfailing knowing, an unfailing Love. The Self.

The Self was—and as years went by, I knew *is*—the unswerving focus of Guides that come through Mataare. More than any other single thing, the transmissions have always been about Identity and the journey of Identity: who we think we are and who we think the Other is. The realization is: I am the Other. We are One.

I cannot speak for your life, but in mine, this represented a fundamental departure in my mind and heart, which, once adopted, would prove to have cataclysmic implications. Simply said: It changed everything.

The more I worked the concept, the more it worked me. Session after session, whether a spoken highlight or simply an underlying premise, I learned of the Self and how to make it active in my life.

When I met the Guides through Mataare, I had been a member of a meditation community for over twenty years. I have never stopped meditating; my incomparable Guru is my teacher to this day.

Gurus and masters play an indispensable role in the evolution of individual souls and of our planet. They hold the Light, incarnate—and our feet to the fire. They are adepts and the practice of meditation they teach us is foundational and life-changing. My Guru saved my life.

The Guides brought me something else. They brought me Love, unconditional, unreasonable, un-interruptible, huge. Love without judgment. It resides in them. It is dynamic in them. When I encountered them all those many years ago, there they were in the middle of a field of Love and I knew it. They taught me from there.

The Guides have a defined purpose: to bring the self to the Self. In a very real, perceivable way, they made me my own guru. That is their job, as defined by them: to make us Sovereign. It is a long journey.

This book, *Merlin: In His Own Words*, is the first of a series—or so I hope. Those hundreds of tapes I alluded to represent dozens upon dozens of voices. So it is my hope that this first book will soon be joined by *Sun Bear: In His Own Words*, *Phylos: In His Own Words*, and so on.

Each of these voices is a prism through which to touch the Divine through ones who touch the Divine at will—the Guides. Guides are already one with God. God's Will is already their will. They *are* the God-infused state.

As Phylos, Keeper of Akasha, once told me, "We Guides have no will of our own. We have only God's. That means we have no choice. We can only serve the Divine because we are that Will. And that is the source of a constant joy."

It is such a thrill to share the wisdom, grace, and humor of Mataare's Merlin with you—through this small volume that I started 14 years ago that magically came together in the past three weeks. I am grateful.

In Love with you,
Gwendolyn
Portland, Oregon
2007

EDITOR'S NOTE

The material for the channeled content of this book was transcribed from tapes of Mataare during his sessions with groups. It has been edited for grammar, syntax and consistency of form in order to bring greater clarity to the written word, within each chapter and across the book.

In several cases, a given topic that was discussed across several group sessions has been placed in a single chapter in order to reduce redundancy and present a more coherent treatment of that subject. This particularly applies to *Chapter 5: The Path of the Old Soul.*

If we made any errors in the editing of this book, please know that we apologize and they were unintentional.

THE SWAN

This clumsy way of living that moves
lumbering as if in ropes through what is not done
reminds us of the awkward way the swan walks.

And to die, which is a letting go
of the ground we stand on and cling to every day,
is like the swan when he nervously lets himself down

into the water, which receives him gaily
and which flows joyfully under
and after him, wave after wave,

while the swan, unmoving and marvelously calm,
is pleased to be carried, each minute more fully grown,
more like a king . . . farther and farther on.

Rainer Maria Rilke
(*translated by Robert Bly*)

ONE

MY NAME IS MATAARE

Mataare Introduces Himself & Channeling

Hello. My name is Mataare. That is not my birth name. My birth name was Paul McClain. "Mataare" is the name I have been given by Spirit.

Even though I do a lot of channeling and other things that many people would consider New Age, I am not really a New Age person. My background is not in metaphysics. I never considered myself open to the whole metaphysical and spiritualist realm. I tended to be, and still tend to be, skeptical of non-physical things. My tendency is to approach life in a linear manner. But that is getting extremely difficult these days.

I used to pride myself on having a linear, engineering type approach to life. And now people that I'm closest to are telling me, "Man, you're such a space case." This is hard for me. I want to say, "But you don't really know me. That is not the real me." Although I have a friend who knew me before I did this work and he tells me, "You can't keep saying this isn't your background because it's been twenty-five years now."

What I do is called *channeling*—channeling Spirit Guides. It has also been called a *séance* and any number of other names. I'll explain a little about what this is and how it works for me.

Spirit, which is *the What* we are going to be working with, is an intelligent, conscious energy that is around everybody and around everything. It is drawn to you in a number of different ways. It is drawn to you by the kinds of feelings and thoughts you have, the kind of things you believe in and don't believe in, and the kinds of things you aspire to. Your every thought and feeling tends to create an ambiance around you that is, I believe, simply an electromagnetic force that draws to you a like or complementary kind of energy.

Amongst that energy that you draw may be friends and relatives of yours who have died and gone on to a different state of being. Yet some part of them may be around you. They may not be around you in the sense that you here are around each other. But, on the level of a more subtle field, they may be in touch with your consciousness in some way—even if they have passed over to the other side—that is, if they are available to you and available to Earth.

They do not need to be friends and relatives. They can be people, or a consciousness, that you have never met before, but they may have had a similar life lesson as you have had. And it may be a part of their path to facilitate somebody else who has had a common experience.

The Spirit world, at least amongst the realm called *Guides*, is a helpful force, one of the more positively influencing forces that people can be in touch with because that realm is very altruistic.

People want to know. "Why do Guides do it? Why do they help?" And their answer would probably be something like, "What else is there to do?"

Really! This work is a part of their path—part of a Guide's path.

Guides can include historical figures, religious or spiritual figures, healers, doctors, farmers. In the Spirit world, if you have something to offer and you are willing, it's a part of your path to help the lives here. That is how you end up with a spirit influence that surrounds you.

You can also attract it because you believe in certain figures or spiritual forces, so that your belief in those spiritual forces makes you interactive with it.

The beliefs that I'm speaking of are fundamental, and they underlie whatever one's more superficial beliefs are. For example, if you're an atheist or agnostic and you don't believe in any kind of a Spirit world, you don't believe you need to have a Spirit Guide. You may simply be a person who is humanistically oriented; you don't believe there's any force greater or beyond yourself. But if your heart and mind are open and helpful—and that is a fundamental belief—that may draw a spiritual influence, whether or not you believe in it.

On the other hand, if you have a lot of anger towards that kind of consciousness or toward people who believe in that kind of thing, that also reflects a certain underlying belief and attitude that is attractive to certain kinds of spirits and influences, either positive or negative.

I don't claim to know how it all works. I don't fully understand these things. But all of these ways of feeling and thinking—some that I can't even imagine or describe—all reflect a state of being. And that state of being interconnects with unseen forces that ultimately further our development.

That's what I've come to believe and that's what I understand. You may understand it a little differently, and the Guides will explain things in their own way too.

A lot of these forces and energies aren't human beings or even ex-human beings. A force can be a field of light or a higher consciousness. Some of the beings that come through are angels or angelic beings. Others may be a consciousness connected to elemental forces. For example, the wind and similar forces have a consciousness that is different from what we might consider consciousness. And these elemental forces, when they come through a medium such as myself, may feel perfectly comfortable describing themselves as fairies, elves, leprechauns, devas, dakinis, pixies, gnomes, sylphs . . . all kinds of things.

They will use whatever paradigm people can identify with to describe something about their nature; they will use some manner of paradigm we can understand. They don't really seem to have any identity issues! Anything that resembles what they are, they're fine and go with. Their main thing isn't about *who they are* but *what their message is*. And, usually, they have some very helpful things to say.

Now what is a *medium*? If a medium is present, and there are people who want to hear what the Spirit world has to say, then the Spirit will take some form that is understandable to the people who want to hear.

Mediums fall into all different ranges and capacities. In the spiritualist sense, a medium can be a channeler or trance medium who speaks voices from the Spirit world. But sometimes the medium for a Spirit can be an animal that tries to communicate something to you. Or the medium can be your own thoughts. Your thoughts may serve as a medium to the Spirit. You may get a flash of an idea. If a person is open and a Spirit wants to communicate and there is a viable medium, they may communicate.

Not every Spirit has messages that are in spoken words or language. A medium for Spirit could be art or writing or music—some creative sort of expression. Spiritual force does not necessarily express itself through spoken language that has some intellectually grasp-able message. Many things that they want to get across may not have to do with any sort of mental notion. It may have to do with forms of awareness other than mental concepts.

What I do is channeling; I'm a channel. The Spirits like to use me for the purpose of communicating their messages; and they will speak in a language that we can understand. They speak the language that I know: English. Even though some of the Spirits may come from other parts of the world, they have to speak in a language that I'm familiar with initially. So they will speak in English although they may feel like they're speaking in their language. Often times they will ask you if you understand them because *they* do not fully understand the words that are coming out. They will understand you too.

Really, the thing that they project is telepathic. I am the translator. And a good medium is one who can be flexible enough for the Spirits to be able to get their message across.

I seem to be able to do that, although I don't consider myself to be especially spiritually-evolved, any more than the next person. I don't believe that Spirit necessarily looks for some specially-gifted person or being. They just look for people who are open in some way; and if the person is willing, then they will work with them. And if I am also willing to change and to grow, I can benefit from the fact that they come through.

I have benefited by the fact that the Spirits have come through me over the years, but I didn't go to Tibet and sit on a mountain, and nobody touched me from the sky. I didn't have anything like that. It doesn't really work like that. A lot of times people who develop any sort of psychic aptitude are, more often that not, extremely troubled at some point in their lives—often going back to childhood.

I found that most of the psychics I know who are worth their salt have had an extremely disturbing childhood. Something about wanting to get out of this world either gets you out of this world or insane. One or the other. Or maybe they're the same thing.

And so, I guess it serves to re-balance that person if his or her approach is open or humble. Although mine certainly wasn't—and isn't—humble. I learned the hard way, let's just say.

When all of this started happening with me, I didn't really believe in any of it. I remembered *that* years after I became fascinated. Once this opening started, I began to remember that I had had a lot of experiences as a child that I thought were dreams.

One of the experiences I had was continuously finding myself out of my body. *All the time*. Only, as a child, I didn't realize that I was going out of my body. Lots of times it would happen just prior to waking up in the morning. I was thinking that I was either half-awake or half-asleep. But I'd be aware of what everybody in my household was doing. We lived in a three-floor house and I could see people—I could see my family and what they were doing even though I was lying in bed.

At one point I started to notice that if I moved too much, I would leave my bed and float through the wall. I also noticed that I didn't have any real control over what was happening. I thought I was just sort of *imagining it*, imagining things. Then I started telling my family—what they were doing, what they were eating, and things like that. As a child I thought I was constructing this by the sounds that I heard. That's what made sense to me.

I had a lot of unusual experiences until I was about eleven years old; and then they all went away.

I had four siblings: one older sister and three younger brothers. My older sister was a vegetarian. She was into wheat germ and magic, and she was very, very interested in what was happening to me. I thought she was crazy. I couldn't identify with her. I couldn't relate to her. And I began to think this whole thing was just a lot of nonsense. I disassociated from her.

But at some point in my teenage years, I heard on the radio about a woman who showed people how to journey outside of their bodies. Even though I didn't know it then, that was a familiar trigger for me. She called herself a *guru*. So I figured, "Maybe I should find myself a guru." But when I found a guru, I also found out that doing stuff like journeying outside your body was frowned on. And so I frowned on anything like that too.

What I learned from this particular guru was how to meditate and that meditation was for peace and to feel a sense of connectedness. That was all I wanted, anyway. I didn't want to know about God. I didn't want to know about anything else. I just wanted a little peace of mind because I was insane.

At some point, I fell in love with meditating. I meditated for years, but it was not a major part of my life for very long. I was very into it for a couple of years. And then, years later, it was just a part of my life.

Then some strange things began to happen that I did not at the time connect with meditation. But that is the only connection I can make now.

I had been meditating for seven or eight years and nothing really strange had ever happened up to then. Then I started to leave my body. I would get relaxed so that I would either fall asleep or meditate and then *pshum*!—I would feel myself fly out of my body. I was scared to death to go to sleep. Scared to relax. Scared to do anything because I didn't feel like I had any control. It actually felt like something was pulling me out and I was scared to death.

Because the little background that I had with meditation through this particular guru considered leaving your body a bad thing, I thought I was a bad person. I thought I had done something wrong. It really scared me to death.

At the same time, I also started to have dreams where people—I called them the *dream people*—would come and talk to me and sort of calm me down. They would tell me about my life and help me sort things out. That was very helpful. But I never knew what was going to happen—whether I would have this frightening experience of going out of my body or just fall asleep normally and have nice dreams.

Then things began to get stranger and stranger. I started hearing things that were not going on in the room and seeing things that it did not appear anyone else could see. And when I talked with people, with friends or family or whatever, a strange thing started to happen. It was as though their physical voices would fade into the background and I would start hearing something other than what they were saying. I didn't realize at the time what was going on. So I'd start responding to what I thought they were saying and people got very upset.

I would tell them things that were a response to what they were *feeling and thinking* but not to what they were really saying. People felt invaded. So I had all this reactivity going on from people, and I just thought I was going insane.

So I went to sign myself into a mental institution. If you are familiar with New York (which is where I'm originally from), I was going to a big, famous hospital called Bellevue. It was the only one I knew. I thought that maybe I could get some help there. *This was a very important moment for me.*

As I was getting off the train, I ran into a friend of mine whom I hadn't seen for years. I started talking to him, telling him these things that were going on. I told him that I was going to see if I could talk to somebody at Bellevue and get some help. His eyes opened up so wide! He said, "Don't do that. Don't do that!" He told me that he had just gotten out. Just released! He said, "You don't want to tell them about this."

So he redirected me to Weiser's, a very famous bookstore in New York, full of metaphysical books, which, as I said, I was not into at all. But I went anyway. That store was overwhelming, huge! There were volumes and volumes of things I had no interest in. On the way out of the store, I saw a bulletin board covered with the business cards of psychics and lots of other New Age stuff.

One card stood out so I thought that I'd talk to that psychic. Maybe there was some truth to some of this past-life stuff, I thought. I went to see her and she recommended that I go see a friend of hers who was a trance medium. So I went to see this guy and he goes, "Oh you're not going insane. You're just slipping into trance." And I said to myself, "There you have it: I'm insane!"

Then he channeled for me and some of the dream people came through. One of them told me his name. It was the same person I had talked to in my dreams. He told me that I was a channel. Then he asked me if I wanted to channel. I told him, "No! In fact, I would just like all of this all to stop!!"

The dream person said fine, and a few other things, and left.

And it stopped. Week after week went by, and month after month. I started to miss the dreams, the unusual experiences. I felt very lonely. You know, I had already alienated everybody in my life!

So I went back to this guy. I thought he stole the dream people from me. He went back into trance, and I told the dream people that I'd like them back. I also told them that I didn't want to go into these states when I didn't want to. So they taught me how to go into trance when I wanted to, and how to stay out of trance when I wanted to.

I don't know why I didn't think of that before or why they didn't suggest that before. But they are like that! If you don't ask, they don't say. And even if you do ask, they still may not say.

I cannot figure them out. I used to think they confused me on purpose, but now I know that they just have a different orientation. It seems they do not relate in the same ways we relate. I'm beginning to understand at least that much. But I cannot get a hook on how they do relate, except to say that they do try to help us.

At any rate, one of the things they suggested was for me to do these channelings once a week, or once every two weeks, and to do it at the same time every time. In that way, they would get to know the cycle and would come at that time. And so I would channel at a certain time and then stop it. I was like a cow that needs to get milked. That is still what it feels like to me.

So they would come at those times and they wouldn't come at other times. And they suggested I just do the channeling with friends that I felt comfortable with. And then they laughed. They started laughing! Now I know why—they knew it was never going to stay with just "friends I felt comfortable with."

Friends tell friends who tell other friends. And so it's twenty-five years now I've been doing this. I travel around the country and do this. *And I just love it!*

It's a very different experience for me now than it was in the beginning. I love channeling. I love doing this. And it is remarkable how it shifts my life. Things that may seem ordinary to other people seem very, very big to me. Just coming here today, I had a series of mishaps like you would not believe.

I guess people have a lot of preconceptions about the Spirit world. They sort of figure, for example, that if a person is *with* the world of Spirit, that person would be healed physically. I am continually asked, "Why do you get sick?" And I cannot understand why people would think I wouldn't get sick. I'm a human being. I get sick.

People also think, "If you're psychic, you should know everything." Now where do people get that impression? For me it's the Spirit beings who are psychic. I know what I know. And I don't know what I don't know. And I don't know *why* I know the things I know, or how to get to know what I want to know. What comes, comes! What doesn't, doesn't! That's exactly the way I found things to be.

I have not been able to get to the things that I want to know just because I want to know them. I have not been able to stay healthy, and *I really want to stay healthy.* And other times, I haven't gotten sick when I thought I would.

It really doesn't work like that, at least not for me. There are a lot of people who associate their spiritual development with how healthy they are mentally or physically. But as far as I know, some of the most powerfully spiritually-aware people I know seem to have major stuff going wrong in their lives. Not all of them, but some.

It seems to me that the Spirit world comes to the people who need it. A lot of times, Spirit comes to the people who need it the most. I feel like my Spirit Guides and Teachers saved my life. The fact that I'm still alive is a miracle to me, considering where I came from. So mine is a very different point of view.

I never related to anything like "Spirit comes to somebody because they are so-called 'spiritually high.'" Spiritually bankrupt, perhaps. Spiritually desperate, yes. Maybe those are the people who draw Spirit to them.

I think a lot of the things that happen that I don't understand come (and came) from a twisted way of functioning that led to twisted results in my life. That's what the Spirits are helping me to gradually unravel. For me, this is a miraculous experience. I haven't found it anything other than that. But I also know that for other people it may be different.

So now we're going to invite the Spirits to come. I'll do an invocation, followed by a prayer of protection that comes from the Kabala, an ancient Hebrew mystical text. And then I will invoke different names of God from different cultures and different languages.

I do the prayer of protection because many of us are very psychically open. And when you are open and there is a lot of psychic charge around, you are open to things you don't necessarily want to be open to. So I always do a prayer of protection when I do a group. In that way, if you have any psychic or spiritual experiences as a result of the boost that seems to happen when the Spirits come around, those experiences will be of the kind you would welcome.

Now when I say the prayer of protection, repeat the words after me. After the prayer of protection, we'll do seven Oms. Oms are like this: OOOhhhhmmmm. Do your best to match my pitch. The sound of this kind of *om* is a way to unify the energy more than the traditional *Au-uhmmm* they say in India. Although that's fine too, the *om* we do is more like a tuning exercise, like an orchestra tuning up. The Guides use this similar vocal frequency to home in and then come through on.

So even if you're a bit tone deaf, just make the sound and do your best to match my pitch. But do utter some sound. That is how the Spirits connect in the way needed for me to go into trance.

I'm in trance generally an hour and a half to two hours. If you need to leave early, that's fine. If you need to use the bathroom or leave early, it's best to go while the Spirit is talking. Don't go until the Spirits are in and have started talking. Do not get up and move around just because there is a pause and I am slumped over. That's *not* the time to move around. Once the Spirits start talking, you can move around or leave if you need to.

Now, this is not going to be a spooky kind of experience, even though I'll be doing this with the lights off. It's going to be just like talking to me, except a little different. But there are no unusual phenomena. Nobody floats. My head doesn't spin around.

The Spirits will come into my awareness and integrate with me the best they can. Some are better at that than others. One of the things that may happen is sometimes they may flop around in the chair. That doesn't tend to happen too much. Or, you may hear some grunting, groaning, throat clearing, or singing as they try to get used to my body and my vocal range. Some are better at this than others. Generally, it's a smooth transition.

The Spirits sometimes carry something resembling accents, especially if they are from other countries or other parts of the physical universe. The reason for the accents is not because they've learned to speak English in a funny way. Rather it's because they seem to retain some of the music and the syntax of their native language. And so, even though English is what comes out, they may have something resembling an accent, nonetheless.

But they will all speak in English. (I hope.) It is easier for them to do that, and in a way more difficult. But there was once one Spirit in a private session who liked to speak Latin. He only spoke it to one certain priest. Another Spirit spoke Japanese. That was very interesting!

You see, Spirits don't like people to get dependent on them or their mediums. Their purpose is to help people find their own connection to the Creator. In fact, they suggested to one priest I used to channel for that he stop coming. But he felt he had vital issues he wanted to talk about. He was a younger priest who hadn't been required to learn Latin. So the guides spoke to him in Latin. Eventually, they got rid of him. He stopped coming.

Then there was the time the Spirits spoke to a group in Japanese for forty-five minutes. Now that was very interesting. It started very slowly and phonetically. Then it took hold. It was a Japanese Spirit from the 19th century. Very interesting. Do you know the game called "Telephone?" You whisper a sentence to somebody and by the time it gets around the room, it is a very different sentence. Well, that's the way it is a lot of times with people, even at these sessions. Everyone has a slightly different interpretation of what they heard or what was said.

That evening, though, when the Guide spoke in Japanese, everyone seemed to agree on what the Spirit had said and meant, even though he didn't speak one word of English! That was very interesting.

I had a friend in the group that night who had a Japanese friend who was a translator. He asked that friend to translate the session. Apparently it took some two years. And he told us that the Guide was speaking a very ancient Japanese dialect that is no longer in existence. Older by far than the 19th century this Guide was supposed to be from.

I don't know why or how that happened. The only thing that I can get from it is that a great deal of the communication is telepathic. Even though they speak, it seems that a lot of what they're getting across is other than what they are saying. It's more in what you are feeling.

Also bear in mind that each of you may hear a personal message from a Guide or two. They may go around the room and give people messages. Or they may simply speak off the cuff.

You are welcome to ask questions. After they say whatever they want to say, they will usually ask for questions. It is a good idea to keep your questions to the subjects they have addressed.

Guides are sometimes very psychically aware and very knowing, but they are *not* omniscient. They may know you. Or they may not know you. They may surprise you with what they know about you. And they may surprise you with what they don't know about you too. I've learned that there are just some things they don't care about, and there are other things that they do care about. Sometimes, it's a strange set of priorities. I say that sincerely.

For example, one man came and the Guides didn't seem to know how his wife had died. They knew she was dead, but they didn't know *how* she had died. (In fact, she had committed suicide by a drug overdose.) And although they addressed whatever it was that he needed to have addressed, this very peculiar fact of how she died you would think they would know. But they didn't know. There are so many instances like that. The Spirits know certain things. And they don't know other things you would think they would know. It's a very different way of seeing the universe.

So keep your questions to the subjects that they're addressing—unless they open the session up for more personal kinds of questions. Part of what enables the Spirits to stay here in a gathering is the group's interest. If the discussion gets too focused on one person, it may be very interesting to that person but no one else may be able to make a connection. So, if the Spirits who come start talking to you about things going on in your own personal life, feel free to respond in kind. But don't go on and on with them about it.

Now, *they* may have a tendency to go on and on. If they do, I suggest every one listen very carefully. A lot of times a question may be more than one person's question. That tends to be the case when the Spirits answer very thoroughly. They are aware of other related questions in the room and they'll start answering various permutations. You may think, "I didn't ask all that!" But they're talking to other people as well.

And if they start staring at you, I suggest you listen *very* carefully even if they're not your Guides, and even if it was not your question. If they start staring at you, wake up if you're falling asleep because *they're trying to get something across.*

Okay. I guess that is about it. So, if you'll take a deep breath and then stretch and sigh (Ahhhhhh).

I'm looking around for a moment now to let your faces get impressed on me. That way, if I go completely out, when I come back it's not so much of a shock seeing people. Okay.

So let's do one more stretch and sigh. Ahhhhhh.

Spirit of Light and of Truth, inspire our minds and fill our hearts with love. Heal and energize our bodies and receive our thanks for the many gifts we've been guided towards. We ask to be guided on our paths that we might serve the Most High.

(Now this is the prayer of protection, so please repeat it after me.)

Holy art Thou, Lord of the Universe. Holy art Thou whom Nature hath not formed. Holy art Thou, the Vast and the Mighty One. Lord of the light and of the darkness. O Adonai. Alohim. Tetragrammaton. Allah. Brahma. El. Yahweh. Jehovah. Abba. Mutair. Mut. Quan Yin. Be with us. Amen. Salah.

Now do seven Oms along with me. I may not finish the seven but I'll need you to do at least seven. Then there will be a little pause and then the Spirits will come.

TWO

WHY ARE YOU HERE?

Greetings to all my friends who gather here. I am very happy to come and speak with you.

I am called Merlin, although Merlin is not really my name. My name is actually *Ambrosias*—Merlin Ambrosias of Kelton. That is where I'm from: Kelton. It no longer exists. "Merlin" is a title more than anything else. The proper title is actually *Merlinius* or *Myyrrddin*, depending upon the dialect. But I have come to be spoken of, by those of you who remember me, as *Merlin*.

Merlin is a title given to those who achieve, one might say, a certain level of Druidship, the religion I practiced in my day. It was a universal and somewhat esoteric type of religion that honored not only the Spirit in all things but the geometric and mathematical relationship of all things that exist.

But I have not come to speak to you of these things, good friends. I have come to speak with you of why you are here—*why you are here* in this world. And where exactly is this world anyway? And where are you?

This world is simply a speck of nothing in the middle of nowhere, circling around another star that is a speck of nothing in the middle of nowhere, moving through the universe in the middle of nowhere, going nowhere.

So here you are. You are entities that are conscious that you exist. And perhaps you seek to attach some importance to your existence—because to the extent that you are able to attach some relevance to your existence, perhaps there can be meaning for you. Or that is what some of you might think.

Some of you go about attaching relevance to your existence by inventing identities that you magnify until these identities reach a sufficient level for you to like what you have made up about yourselves. And if these identities work constructively amongst your peers and in your life, you think you have found "the meaning of life." You think you have *understood* something. *But have you?*

YOUR RIGHT SIZE

Well, there are those who do something a little more courageous. They seek their place. And that place may be very, very small. And for many, that is too humbling. But what if that small place were your *right size*? And what if being in "right size" puts you in harmony with forces that are designed to show you something—something other than a proclamation you have made up about yourselves and know already?

In this existence, it is advisable to live with extraordinary openness of mind and heart. Now, it will not be easy to keep an open mind and an open heart. Not in this life. Not in this place. It will not be that easy.

If you wish to have an open mind and heart, you must have some sort of awakening, some sort of *experience* in order to be able to see clearly enough—in order to *know*. One might call this experience a spiritual awakening. A *spiritual* awakening does not necessarily mean that you awaken suddenly to the realm of Spirit. It means that there are veils that begin to fall away. That's a spiritual awakening.

And how might we describe the falling away of these veils? In any number of ways. Perhaps some of you may have experienced an insight or a feeling that communicates to you a sense of why you are here. (And this understanding may not necessarily be intellectual.)

Or perhaps some of you have experienced falling asleep and dreaming and being aware in the dream that you are dreaming. Has anyone had that experience? I believe you call it *lucid dreaming*.

In a lucid dream, you are aware that you are dreaming, and therefore you are "awake" in the dream. You are alert, sharp. Perhaps those of you who have had such a dream have then awakened in the classic sense (your eyes have opened) and have found that the alertness, a crystal clarity, the feeling you had in the dream is somehow retained even after you awake. That is a special thing. What does it mean?

> LUCID
> DREAMING

Or perhaps you have had a dream where you thought *within* the dream that you woke up, but you were really still asleep. Has anyone ever had that experience? Where you feel you have awoken in the dream; and then, all of a sudden, at some point, you wake up again? And this time you are *really* awake, but you had thought you already were. Shocking experience, isn't it, for those of you who have had it! Disturbing, because you thought you *were* awake, and then you find you are *just now* awake.

Perhaps you begin to think: "Well, am I really awake *now?*" This question used to disturb Mataare tremendously. He could never be sure. He had a little reality test (as he called it) to find out. He'd jump up and if he kept going up, he realized he must be sleeping. But if he came back down, there was a *possibility* he was awake. But he was never sure. And so he had a number of tests set up like this because he couldn't tell whether he was awake or asleep.

Or some of you have some sort of vague (or perhaps it is clear) memory of having been here before—or of having died before. And perhaps some of you are wondering, "Why would I ever come back?" This is a very important question.

And mind you: come back to what? What is *this* you came back to anyway? And consider this. What if you didn't *come back?* What if, in fact, you *went on* to your afterlife and *this* is your afterlife? You are in it now. How do you know?

And *where* are you anyway?

Some of these kinds of veils lift as you have awakenings. And you must *seek* these awakenings. You must seek them. You must seek the spiritual experience or you will never know why you are here.

I am not speaking of mere philosophical understanding (which may have some importance) or religious doctrine (which may be important too) or spiritual dogma (which may or may not be important). I am speaking of *experience*. And one experience will not be enough. Even though, for some of you, these experiences may come few and far between, you must seek them.

Some of you have heard that upon death, there is a light that will come to you—or you will go to it. Some of you may have felt that light and seen that light while you are here on earth. Perhaps it was in a near-death experience. Or perhaps it was incidental, such as in meditation. And perhaps you have heard that many of your relations who have gone over before you will meet you there. Of course, you may not know this for a fact, but it is true. And these relations urge you to go to the Source, which will be surrounded by light. It's a very powerful experience.

But do you know something else? Many souls never make it there. They never make it to the Light because, before they ever arrive, they are

GOING TO
THE LIGHT

distracted. That's why your relations are there: to urge you to go into the Light because they know the strong possibility that, before you ever arrive, you will be distracted. Not necessarily by demons and denizens of a darker plane, but by false notions and incomplete experiences that will draw you to things that you think are more important.

Strange little things can distract you. A hurt. A slight. Perhaps a slight was given to someone incidentally because you were in an irritated mood one day, and it suddenly occurs to you that you want to amend that. You want to put that right! Or you are distracted by some journey you were supposed to learn about while you were here, but "forgot" to. Or perhaps you left behind a child, or a husband, or a wife, and you feel somehow incomplete.

And so, one way or another, you are led back into the dimension that you can identify with through your beliefs, experiences, and attachments. And the realm you do not identify with is the realm of Light. No matter how compelling its nature, you do not identify with that realm. Maybe you haven't learned enough about how to identify with that Light and therefore you can't go to it.

The very open-minded and open-hearted amongst you may put aside other concerns and say: "Yes, show me the way. I think I want to go there." And you may let go of other things and go a little further.

Do you know that the very same thing happens to you right here on earth? You don't need to die first. Your spiritual friends and elders appear in your physical existence from places you can't even remember and you identify them. You think, "Ah, I feel a connection with you. I *know* you." And they say, "Listen, go to the Light. These things are more important." It is important to get on with your business and move through this plane so that you are able to embrace the Supreme Beauty.

But you have many distractions here. This is not the easiest of worlds, granted. You will have to put aside all of your fears.

The primary spiritual virtue is *courage*. Courage does not mean you will have no fears. It will only cause you to face them—and perhaps to learn by them and grow. And on the other side of fear is light, enlightenment, awakening. An *alertness* happens when you face your fears.

Now some of you may take more time to let go of your fears than others. And *that's* what you're here for: to gather the necessary knowledge, experience, and awareness, sufficient to face and let go of your fears—enough that you are willingly able to embrace the Light as it reveals Itself to you. *Willingly able* to embrace the Love, *willingly able* to embrace the Supreme, *willingly able* to embrace the Creator, and sufficiently able to let go of other things.

The Creator will not reveal Itself to each of you in the same way. You cannot argue with each other about "what is so" and "which is true." You must accept your experience as it is revealed to you, and according to your own understanding. And you must cease the fighting—the fighting with other people's understanding. You must start to see where others are *right*, not wrong.

There is a great deal wrong with everyone's understanding, including your own. But as long as you are fighting with everybody else's understanding, you will never see what is wrong with your own. You can never go home that way. The fighting must stop. You must see where others are *right* and allow yourself to be drawn to the Light. The way home will be shown, and more will be revealed every single day—*if* you're willing to put down the fight.

There will always be a compelling urge in you to fight. It is an instinct. It is an instinct for your very survival. Your *relevance* is at stake, you see.

PUT DOWN
THE FIGHT

But remember, you are in the middle of nowhere, going nowhere, with no importance or significance whatsoever, except what you are able to make up and get others to agree with you about. And all of that must be set aside to put down the fight.

The "fight" is that somebody has attacked your relevancy and you must bolster it. That is the ego working. If you put down the fight you may say, "Hmmm, maybe there is a little truth to what he says." Good. You must be of an open mind, no matter what you've already learned—and of an open heart, no matter how afraid you are. And then an immediate beauty shall reveal itself. That's the awakening!

Time and time again, you will be led to that awakening and you will not see it. You will be led to these awakenings and left with the feeling: "Huh? What is the meaning of all of this?" You won't understand. And this will happen frequently. That is why it is said that the humble are the fortunate. Because time and time again, they who are humble will set aside their fear and put down the fight.

Now I'm going to tell you something about the nature of the Creator which you can choose to believe or not. I come here to share something with you that is *my* experience. Perhaps I can help you not to undergo so much of what I had to undergo.

The Creator—and there is one!—is *not* impartial. All of you who have ever thought that the Creator is not impartial and seems to be favoring some people more than others *are right*! You can certainly be sure that the Creator favors the humble. They're open, you see. The more humble are able to experience more with less, and there is joy, greater joy, in their hearts because of it. You see? Joy is the unmistakable sign of the presence of God. And it increases.

THE CREATOR IS
NOT IMPARTIAL

Now the Creator has not necessarily favored those who are richer than you, or more loved by others than you, or who get more attention than you, or anything else. That's not the kind of favor I speak of. Perhaps you seek some of those things in an effort to gain a certain amount of control over your existence.

I too once sought a great deal of control over my existence because I was convinced that if I could control enough, then those little things that bothered me would cease bothering me.

The trouble with control is that you can't control *everything*. The trouble with thinking that you can is that you get angrier and angrier at the things and persons and circumstances that won't cooperate with you. And that, ultimately, is just about every*one* and every*thing*. And before you know it, you're angry at everyone and everything, for most or all of the time. And nothing makes sense any more.

That's fear. That's the enemy.

You see, the fundamental presumption about control is in error. The fundamental presumption is that the universe is not a safe place. The fundamental presumption is very often even deeper than that: It is the belief that you are God. Now, this idea is very New Age, I know. But I'm not from the New Age. (Many associate me with being of the New Age but I'm not a New Age type. No, no, no! Oh, the New Age is wonderful but it's really the *Old Age*. It's not new at all.) So: while you are a *part* of the All-That-Is, that is a long way from *being* the All-That-Is.

Now this seems very logical to me, but it doesn't seem too logical to many people here. They think that because they are a part of God, that they *are* God! And "as God," they think they have the right to direct the universe around them. And when the universe doesn't cooperate, it's everybody else's fault. It's as much as saying: "I'm the God at work in the universe and these subjects are not cooperating with me."

But who *is* the God? It's as if you were surfing on the Pacific Ocean and riding a wave and thinking: "Ah, I've mastered the ocean. I've mastered the Pacific." That's no mastery! You've ridden one wave! Just try to do that all day. I am certain one of those waves will show you who's the master of the ocean!

That is why human beings try to estab-
lish their relevancy, because the pain of
feeling powerless is too much. Too

| MASTERING THE OCEAN |

much. That is the dilemma. *Powerlessness.* And it is very difficult for human beings to embrace their powerlessness. You do have power. But in the scheme of things, it's really not much. But that's all right. Because here you are. You exist.

The dilemma is that one never seems to find enough power to be happy; the delusion is that if you can control your life sufficiently, you will be happy. As we were telling a friend just the other day, many go to their grave seeking the control that they believe will bring them happiness but never finding it. Your self-sufficiency and independence, even though you are Americans and feel you have a lot, are not quite enough. You must link to that which is far greater than you are.

Much greater than you are!

Your submission to that which is greater allows you to be supported by it. If you wish to swim, you cannot fight the ocean. But if you relax in a particular way, it can support you. And if you learn certain techniques, you can function in it. And if you create particular devices, such as a ship or the like, you may be able to get even more out of it. But that is a long way from being the "master" of that ocean. When you know your *true relationship* to the universe (that which is infinite), that's where the awakening begins. And if you do not learn your true relationship to an infinite existence, the dream continues.

And so you must fervently seek your true and right size. And as you do, more will be revealed to you about that. Each and every day you will learn, you will grow, you will love, and you will understand what you came here for. You will understand it because you will experience it. You will have spiritual experiences. And you will identify with those who have found those experiences and awakenings before you—those who have spoken of those things and written of those things. You will identify with them more and more and more.

| BELIEFS ARE NOT IDENTITY |

When it comes to spiritual experience and spiritual awakening, formulas don't work. Your formulas about how things are or should be will fail you over and over again. This doesn't mean something is wrong. It means something is right! Because your formulas come from the intellect's desire to interpret existence, but existence is without limit. And sooner or later something from beyond what you have interpreted must evidence itself and interrupt your particular formula.

If you hold to your formulas, sooner or later your beliefs will feel like your identity. They will feel like *who* you are. This doesn't mean you should throw away your understandings. What it means is that you must be remarkably open, open of mind and heart, to learn more and be shown more than that which you have understood already about how it all works. And then more even than that.

And not just open enough to have spiritual understanding come into your awareness. Open enough to seek it! That is the spiritual path— the *seeking*.

And how do you seek? Very simply. You open enough to reach out to "something" that you may not even be always certain is there, and you ask for that "something." And you let that "something" reflect the qualities of unconditional and unlimited Love. And then you invite that "something," which is the most expansive feeling, principle, or consciousness you can identify with, to insert itself into your life and show you the way. And you do this daily. Daily!

It's not enough to say, "Well, once I got very sincere and got down on my knees and I prayed and nothing happened!" That's very much like telling me, "Well once upon a time my breath smelled and so I brushed my teeth. Once. And here it is four months later. I did that brushing my teeth business and my breath never got any better." Hmmm.

You must seek day-to-day. And I can promise you this: If you look and are willing to be shown—even if you don't feel particularly capable or able, even if you feel you're blocked, or think you have tried already—if you are just *willing*, "something" will show up, every day, more and more.

But there are things this "something" will not do: It will not put everything in your life in order. And it won't give you the control you seek over your own life so that you can "theoretically" enjoy it. Because the beauty of life is inherent and doesn't require control over your feeling of powerlessness. It requires acceptance of your condition and a willingness to learn.

That willingness to learn is the state of Love called humility. The path to greatness is through humility. *Humility* does not mean that your ego will be entirely put to rest. Some people think that. Some people are terribly, terribly sincere and they understand the problems that occur with the ego. And they think: "Well, I've been on this path for a long time and I'm still disturbed by my self-centeredness and ego and all that sort of thing." And we say: "Yes, what else is new?"

You see, these things need only *diminish* sufficiently so that you can have an experience of the Source. Sufficiently enough to be able to help others. You'll see. Your ego and your problems will not be eradicated so that you can become a saint. They will not disappear so that you can then gain control of your life, or so that you can enjoy your life. They just diminish enough to let the Light of the Spirit flow through you so that you can help others who are suffering. And you will be lifted by *that service*, you see. If you are self-examining and you see where you get in your own way, you can humbly ask for help so that you can be of service to the Supreme.

YOU NEED
TO ASK

Life then isn't about trying to get all your ducks in a row, to get everything in place. It's about: "How can I be useful to the Light, to the Source, to the Creator. How can I do it *today?*" Even when it seems that all life is concerned about is getting just a little more money, just a little more love, just a little more health, just a little more mastery, just a little more control, just a little more knowledge, just a little more, just a little more. . . .

That kind of life can become extraordinarily self-centered, if you haven't noticed. Sooner or later your own obsession with yourself will drive you mad. And you will be begging: "Help! Save me from my own thoughts! They're killing me!" That is really the beginning of the spiritual journey. You beg:

> Save me from my own selfishness and self-centeredness. All I want to do is give. I don't want to wait until I learn all the lessons of my current career and job so that I can move on to something that feels a little more closely aligned with my purpose. And then have to figure out how I can make money at it so that by the time I'm fifty, maybe, I can be doing what I came here to do.

Or maybe you think you'll start at sixty or seventy. *It needs to be right now. Today.* You need to ask:

HUMILITY IS OPENNESS

> How can I be of service to the Light now? What can I let go of now so that the Light of the Spirit can flow through me? So I can live and realize the purpose for which I have come, now?

> Whatever it is that's in the way, remove it so I may go about the business. Because there are many distractions, and I am tired of pursuing time and time again everything that I think I have to—just one more time— for it to turn out one more time again in a similar way. It doesn't work!

> Help me now! Immediately! Right here! Even if I'm not sure anyone is listening or anything is there!

You see, *that's* openness!

And you will need extraordinary openness. Extraordinary openness means enough openness to ask for help *one more time*. Help with the aspects of your own nature that—time and time again—create your own difficulties. You do this *not* so that you can get control over your life so you can theoretically enjoy it, but so you can be useful to the Supreme Love that is at work in the universe. So the Light of the Spirit may flow through you and you won't feel abandoned or cut off.

There are those of you who think you can't feel or see or hear the Spirit world enough. Even if you believe it is there, or even if you have felt it from time to time, or even if you've had extraordinary spiritual experiences—you think you just can't get awake enough. But that's where your hope lies: in your self-examination and in the help of the Supreme. The Supreme will help you with the parts of you that *you* trip over again and again. So that *you can be here now*! And so that Infinite "something" which exists as a resource within you can begin to flow.

Now if there are any questions you wish to ask of me, I'd be most happy to address your questions and concerns.

Question: I have a question about the relatives that meet you to guide you to the Light. . . .

Merlin: They are relations, but they're not all *blood* relations.

Question: Okay. Where do they come from? Have they made it to the Light? Or not made it to the Light but they want you to because they didn't? Or. . .?

Merlin: Oh, yes, usually they've made it over and over again. That's something I've left out. Yes, they come from Light. And by the way, so did you! But you may have gotten confused about something somewhere along the line. You are wondering now how to return to it.

I don't want to give anybody the impression that once you make it to the Light, you get to stay there forever. As soon as you get the point, the Creator inasmuch says, "You got it? Yes? Yes! Now, get out and do something with it!"

That's the purpose of going into the Light. "You get it yet? Yes? Yes! Remember it—and go! There are sick, suffering souls who are looking for me. Go and get them!" And so out you go. You think I'm joking?

Now many of you think you did something wrong because you have some sort
of vague memory of that: "I know there's

a home. I feel it. I've been there. How do I get back? Did I make a mistake?" I am certain you made a mistake. But that has nothing to do with why you are not there. It's totally irrelevant. We all make mistakes—over and over again. None of us has found that we've ever become perfect, flawless. The Source of this existence—believe it or not—is extraordinarily permissive. *That is why so much that you don't like can go on down here!*

The Source of this existence does not hold to the fear that something is wrong with the system. It doesn't hold that fear. There is hurt. There is pain. There is suffering. But people must awaken. Souls must become awake to embrace the Light.

The Creator is a lover of agencies, you see. I'm not certain exactly why. But the Creator seems to be happy only if there are entities will-ing to be an agency. As a lover of agencies, the Source of this exis-tence likes to work *through* things.

Now I know that for me this has been a great benefit. If the Creator wasn't a lover of agencies, I don't know what I'd do! But since the Creator *is* a lover of agencies, and I happen to be an agency, I feel very loved. I know what I'm doing in my existence.

There isn't a doubt about it in my mind—most of the time. There are some doubts which occur to me rather shockingly and surpris-ingly, every now and then: a thing I thought I'd learned and I didn't. It's very, very true. Yes, the most extraordinary and unsuspected things just keep showing up. Baffling. Baffling. I've come to enjoy it.

So, the Source of existence is not the kind of being or entity which invites beings into death—but into eternal life. Now, some people think that eternal life means a glorious place or experience or dimension where one reaches some ultimate level and then never has to do anything anymore. But that is some projection that comes from their pain, their long struggle. They imagine that what will be their relief is an eternal rest of some kind.

But that is death! That's stagnation! *Creator is that which transcends Its nature constantly*. That's what *Infinite* means. If It did not transcend Its own nature, would that not imply that it would be *finite*? The Source is in a constant process of translation—a constant process of transcending Its own nature.

Those of you who have determined that you are made in the image of that Creator might realize that there's a part of you that will constantly seek to transcend your nature. And you are given that opportunity to transcend, constantly. And it *is* an opportunity. It doesn't have to be a struggle.

Look, it isn't easy. But it's very rewarding. This is not the easiest place to do it, you may have discovered. There are easier places to do it. But then why do those of us who come here in my fashion (and many other fashions) come here? Why aren't we dwelling in those easier places, so to speak, minding our own business? There must be something beautiful that we prefer about places such as this. And that beautiful thing is: It's our opportunity to pass on what was passed to us. You see? This is where we move forward.

What would we do if there were no more beings reaching out? I don't know. I haven't found that existence yet. I don't know that I want to.

What I do know, from my communion with the Source, is that this is what has resulted for me. This coming here and doing many other things in many other places is what has resulted. So now I don't have to make a great number of plans anymore. I'm shown. And I look. And I ask. And it's beautiful!

It is not easy. But I don't struggle. *We* never struggle. It is work! In fact we call it *the Great Work*. It is beyond all of us. Far beyond me. That's why I have a connection with the Infinite, you see.

If I could give you the most helpful information, I would say to cultivate a contact with the Source. Refine that connection, and serve that connection.

> THE GREAT WORK

Now! You don't have to become "perfect" before you can do it.

Some have a *too* spiritual approach to things. Hippocrates may indeed have said something like, "physician, heal thyself." Very wise for a physician. But at the time I think he was trying to insult the person he was speaking to. However, let us not make that demand with spirituality.

If you wait to serve your Source until you become "spiritual"—whatever that means—you'll be waiting a very long time. Instead, don't wait! Serve now! Many times, over and over, to the maximum degree, compulsively and obsessively until you have nothing left. And, at the end of that road, a light can fall on some of us.

The very nature of the intense and sensual plane you're in is so dynamic that many other things catch your attention. But it's very, very simple. Ask for help. Develop a connection. Refine that connection. Serve that connection. Very simple. And you will experience extraordinary synchronicity. Beauty.

Perhaps you call them *miracles*.

THREE

✳

WAKING UP

Now, I'm just curious. Is there anyone here who knows precisely why they have been born? Is there anyone here who has thought about that at all? I think yes. Is there anyone here who's a little bit obsessed with that? Yes? Is there anyone here who's sort of given up on trying to figure that out?

Well, when was it you were born anyway? Somebody told you that you were born on a particular date—and for those of you who have very accurate records—at a particular moment. And for those of you who have good memories, maybe you even remember being born. Does anyone here remember the moment of their birth? Anyone here have those kinds of memories?

So none of you really remember specifically when you were born, but you know that you must have been born. Yes? Perhaps you've seen other people being born and perhaps you figure since they were born in a particular way, and these things have been studied and such, you feel you must have been born in much the same way. Yes?

But when was that first originating moment? I wonder if you can remember that? Was it at conception? Was it prior to conception? Was it at birth? Was it at two years old, or three, or five? Can anyone here remember their first moment of cognizance? Anyone?

All that you know is that somewhere along the line, you "came to." Yes? Now, is there anyone here who is not convinced they've "come to" yet? Because if there are those amongst you who are not convinced you've come to yet, you're on the right track. You see? Because what is happening is: you're in a *process of* "coming to."

And what are you "coming to" to, by the way? What? What are you waking up to? And when you are fully awake, what shall it be like? What will you do?

And you are waking up, truly waking up. There are significant moments of awakening. Perhaps you can remember a few of those. Perhaps you might remember particular points. Now moments of awakening are oftentimes exhilarating. They are peak moments. But sometimes they're terribly difficult. There are painful and tragic moments which have served as awakenings for some of you. Has anyone had one of those, or a few of those, in the course of their life? Very painful awakenings?

Has anyone here had a particularly joyous awakening, an ecstatic awakening that you're sort of looking to return to again? Because, you know, they tend to disappear. Is anyone amidst an awakening right now? Yes? Someone said yes? Ahhh.

Yes, you see, after a while, after a few awakenings, that state of being never goes away entirely. It never entirely goes away. Maybe the peak is off, but it's very difficult to go entirely asleep again. Have you found that out? Have any of you ever *tried* to go back to sleep because you were convinced that whatever it was you awoke to was a mistake? That there was no place you could apply it, or nothing you could do with it, and it was a most annoying state of being. And what did you do about that? Did you do your best to try and forget it—and then did you become angry that you couldn't let it go? And did you think: "What did I have it for if it doesn't mean anything?" Anyone ever been there?

So, it's all just a matter of waking up. And what exactly are you waking up to? *What* are you waking up to? What is there *worth* waking up to?

Well, I think one thing worth waking up to is Love. What is the point of waking up if you're miserable in that state? Some of you have become alert and been miserable too. You've perhaps woken up to a particular extent and then been lonely too long. Or you've woken up to a particular extent and then been let down, or hurt, or disappointed. And that is something very, very powerful—because after you've been let down, then how do you keep going forward? Why should you keep going forward? It takes a great deal of courage and it takes a great deal of commitment

And very often, you can't do it alone. You'll have to get together with other persons and try to do it collectively. Either with groups or with partners, or both. Now, when you have to find partners, it can be particularly troublesome—because you can't get your partners to do what you want them to do. Now, you might say, "But I would never try to get my partner to do what I want. That's not the point. I understand that. We love each other in an unconditional way. We're unconditionally supportive of each other." Or perhaps you're with someone with whom there is great love, but your paths seem to conflict in some form or another.

Well, did you know that romance is peripheral to the soul's intention? That's right. The soul wants to get down to business, you see. The soul just wants to get on with what it came here to do. And there's a very funny thing that happens then; and I'd like to talk about it a little bit.

OLD SOULS

You see, the soul (if you are an old soul) is going to be very challenged. Because if you're an old soul, you did not save the *easiest* issues for your last incarnations. In fact, you avoided the most difficult issues and so they wind up in your last incarnations. And that's part of the reason why, if you're an old soul, it sometimes seems like such a struggle.

This is very, very baffling to souls who are old souls. Old souls tend to get very jealous of their younger brothers and sisters because old souls are busy working on themselves, doing spiritual things, evolving, and being quite serious, and high-minded, and loving, and forgiving. And then they see those bratty young souls not doing any work on themselves and getting all the goodies. The old souls think, "I do all the work and they get all the fun."

I'm not making a joke. I run into this *all* the time. I come through Mataare a great deal and people say, "Listen, Merlin . . ." (generally, they try to be very respectful, but I can tell they're seething with anger, and that's all right. But basically, they say things along the lines of:) "...I've done everything. I've either read about it, or you've told me something. I followed this prescription or that prescription. I'm doing all this..." (and they try to gently and humbly approach me and they say:) "What am I doing wrong?"(but, meanwhile, in their mind they feel they've got us—because they know they've done everything and anything we said, they're going to say:) "I've done that already." (You see? And really what they're saying is: "There is no reason why it should be like this. And I really want to know what's going on. Is this all real? Am I being ripped off? Is it all a fake?"

You see?

All of these things have to do with growth. And their approach to growth and enlightenment is, "If I'm a good boy, or if I'm a good girl, don't I get a cookie?" "If I do A, B, and C, don't I get a reward? Because that is what I want. That's why I'm doing A, B, and C. I want my reward!" But it really doesn't work like that. It is not about *work equaling a reward*. It is about beauty. It is about growth. But it isn't about A plus B, etc. And I will tell you why.

In the three-dimensional world, there's a certain kind of energy that makes you very successful. The three-dimensional world tends to be very competitive, if you hadn't noticed; and the better competitors get more of the goodies. That's generally how it seems to work. You might have noticed it's like that in nature too—the survival of the fittest.

But there are some more sophisticated and enlightened beings who are *not* competitive. They maybe used to be. But the great survivors are those that create a cooperative existence, not a competitive one. Competitors, you see, only rule until a better competitor comes along.

You might take, as an example, the shark. The shark is a very good survivor, isn't it. But the shark is a very young species, compared to the age of the earth. Take another example: the dinosaurs. They were plant eaters. Look how long they survived. They were here for millions of years. How long have the sharks been here? Perhaps 25,000 years in this current form? But you don't know how long they'll survive.

Now let's look at human beings. This recent collective of civilization, both Eastern and Western, has lasted roughly six or seven thousand years. It's in its infancy. You don't know how successfully Eastern and Western civilization will emerge if it remains competitive. Something has to shift—because there is a higher way of functioning than that of a rigorous, competitive existence. A much higher way.

And that higher way is a *higher dimensional* way. Let's call it a fourth dimensional way. In a fourth dimension of existence, a different set of energetics is needed to be happy. And certain other things are no longer required. For example, a competitive existence is self-centered, fueled by a need for survival. And underlying the competition, driving it, is a great deal of fear.

Perhaps the highest form of third dimensional survival would be something like: I win, you win. You know this kind of agreement. The question might be, "What can I do where I can be satisfied at the same time you're going to be satisfied?" In that way, both entities are satisfied. But this is still very self-centered because: "If I don't win, I don't like it; and I'm only giving you a win so I can win too." This is very self-centered.

One of the reasons self-centered is not good (and I'm not moralizing) is due to the kind of energy that drives it. When a being becomes very self-focused, it's usually out of the fear that they won't get something or they might lose something. Underlying all competition is a very anxious drive to claim and get. And this anxious, fearful drive turns in on itself after a while. Competition is very narrow and very closed. It's not open; and it's an inefficient survival modality.

On a higher dimensional plane, however, there is another way to function. In this higher plane of functioning, the thought is more like this: "What can I do to give?" And the reason that such a thought can come forward is because it's based on an understanding of an *Infinite Well*.

It isn't because that person has thought, "What is kind? What is moral? What is right?" It's because that person has touched a limitless place in their experience that has changed their underlying feeling from that of *need* to that of *supply*. Therefore, they are not driven by need or desperation.

To come to a higher dimensional existence, a person—a being—must seek that experience. It is not enough to believe. It's not enough for me

> AN INFINITE
> WELL

or anyone to come along and say, "There is an infinite supply, so believe it and affirm it," because that will never address the deepest fear. It may sound good because there's truth to it, but it doesn't address the deepest fear.

When push comes to shove, so to speak, something has to happen where that being, that person, is awakened to *an experience of supply*. So it is incumbent upon the person to search for that experience— to search for the spiritual experience and find it and say, "Yes, I feel it. I see it."

It is from that place of experience that the energy can finally begin to shift and serenity can come into that person. Then quite naturally, and seemingly incidentally, everything begins to come to such a soul as that. Everything that is really important, according to this more pleasant and fulfilling way of being.

At the same time, understand that for lifetimes as a human being, you have been living in the world—and you have been developing patterns of need and drive, and accumulating and taking care of things that you feel you need in order to be secure. Even when you touch upon the Infinite, you're going to have habituated patterns in your psyche that repeatedly do things that rob your soul of energy. And sooner or later, you will have to make a choice to lay down that part of your being—the fight.

We were talking about that earlier, about the fight. To lay down the part of your being that still is fighting, struggling, and scrapping for its existence. And that takes time. The only way you're going to be willing to put down the thing you have been cultivating for lifetimes—the ability to fight, claw, struggle, and win, at any price—is if you develop *trust*.

You did not develop all that orientation to struggle and ambition because you were bad. You developed it because you needed it to survive, and you got hurt when you didn't have it. And so you're not going to easily lay that aside just because now and then you touch a place where there is an Infinite Well and you have a little awakening. You say, "Yes, yes, I understand." And then you're back in the world where you're seeing all the cutthroats and everything else and, when push comes to shove, you're going to think, "Well, I can do that just as well as they can." In fact, you may think, "I can do it better than most." If you are an old soul, you're excellent at it. You see?

So, what is going to make you want to put that down? Well, two things: One, you realize it ultimately doesn't work; and two, you're tired of fighting. So when the stakes begin to rise and the fight escalates and your will is clashing with somebody else's will, it's very likely, if you're two old souls, that sooner or later you'll give it up and you'll forgive each other.

But if you're an old soul fighting a young soul, you're no match. You're no match for those young whippersnappers. They have the energy to conquer the world many times over. They will win, eventually. They have more energy than you over the weeks, the months, the years of battle! That person in the office you've been fighting with will not get tired. They will get worse!!

You're going to be the one that wants to leave. You're going to be the one that wants to quit. You're going to be the one that wants to back off. Because you don't have the energy for all of that continued fighting. It's stupid. It's silly. And soon you're going to start to see it's a waste. It's a big waste of time. It's a waste of energy.

You realize, "I just don't need it. I just don't want it." And you're going to start to see how to put an end to the fight. Your investment in winning is going to be put aside and you're going to start saying things like, "Well, maybe you're right." And years of fighting are over. And you are left with all that energy you never have to expend on fighting. People are going to have to look for somebody else to fight.

Then you will be like a light. They'll probably turn to you and think, "There's something I like about that fellow." Suddenly you appear to be

> ### CARRYING THE LIGHT

this very wise being, you see. Because you just keep side-stepping all the fights—and, as a result, you are left with sufficient energy. Rather than fighting with others, you're able to see signs and clues inwardly and outwardly that are not visible to them because they're too busy trying to work their agendas on the world; they are too busy to notice what's going on around them or within them.

But you are sensitive. Things will flow to you. Things will come to you. Very often, those that are around you will love, help, and support you. You will start experiencing such richness in your life that you're going to start thinking in terms of, "Well, how can I give?" More and more.

Now you won't become a perfect person all the time. You'll still have your personality and your temper from time to time—and all of your personal character traits which have become inculcated and that are not necessarily the most wonderful traits to have. But they will be diminished sufficiently so that they're not creating disharmony and discord everywhere you go.

This is when you will discover precisely why you are here—because more and more, everywhere you go, you will have the privilege of carrying Light, and you won't even know how you did it. You will find that you have become a being of the Light. You will be on a different power source—one that is far more powerful than the drive of angst and fear.

Your soul is here to learn about that Source. That's a part of the business of why you have come. Without the world to fight with, it is relatively easy. It can be challenging sometimes, but it is also relatively easy.

RELATIONSHIPS

But it is not so easy with your intimate partners. Partners you become intimate with go deep down inside you to those untested and raw places where you are very sensitive and where you will truly just want your needs to be met. And though they will be comforts and supportive, sooner or later you will have to find out about a different kind of love, one that is not about getting your needs met.

I know this is not the popular psychology which says that you should be able to have your needs met. Your needs *will* be met. But the relationships you're in are not about getting your needs met, even though your needs will get met. That is not what relationship is about. It's about a discovery of the kind of love you don't know a damn thing about.

Unconditional love is *greater* than what you expected to find. Your expectations and your needs are usually not about that, not about unconditional love.

To put it differently, you are in relationship to learn about unconditional love, but your expectations and needs are about conditional love. You are here to learn about unlimited love. If you try to work out a negotiated, limited, love, such as, "Let's agree. I get this; you get that," you will end up putting a great deal of energy into that and you will get very weary, very quickly. Then love and relationship will be a burden for you.

Maybe you'll get something out of it. But when (not if) that relationship ends, you will end up feeling like, "I will never ever do that again. It's too much work. I don't want one of these contractual arrangements that are growing ever more and more sophisticated and entangled, where eventually my soul is contracted away by all the agreements that I have made in order to negotiate the simple things that I want."

At some point, if love is to grow, to last, and be healthy, I promise you it will become a very different thing. What it will become is something where you will be permanently annoyed with a part of the way your partner is. But you will love that person more and more. You will have preferences. You will wish that certain things about them would change, but you'll quite quickly realize it's probably never going to. And yet a love for them will flow out from you, more and more. You'll have your life, and you'll have their love, and you'll have *your* love.

Sooner or later, you will see that partner go out of his or her way for you in ways that you'll recognize. You will feel, "He/she must really love me." You will see this. And the same thing goes for yourself. You will see yourself behaving in that way not because you negotiated an agreement. You won't know exactly why. It will just come out from you. And the relationship will become something that perhaps you've heard about. It will become a giving—a giving, not a needing. And when people are in a giving state, their problem is not the relationship. The relationship will be just fine. The problems will be other things.

What I have described is a soul mate sort of relationship. Now, first of all, the soul is always mating! But as you would think of them, you must understand: Soul mates do not love each other perfectly. They love each other even with their imperfections. That's what soul mates do.

| SOUL MATES |

Soul mates stop trying to fix each other. Though they may not start out that way. Well, actually, they almost always start out *not trying* to fix each other; then they try to fix each other. And then they quit. They begin accepting; and when they get closer, they try to see if they can still sneak in a little fixing. They try every way they can to fix the other; and because they're soul mates, they just finally give it up.

Sometimes soul mates try to escape from each other. After the period where they try to fix each other, but neither will be fixed, they may say, "Well, I love you but I must move on." But they don't quite exactly move on because what they did when they thought they were moving on was "letting go." And a real love that was always there takes over.

Some of you have been in those situations. I'm not talking about sick and co-dependent relationships where people want to get away but they end up sick and dependent upon each other. That is very destructive. I'm talking about a love relationship that grows deeper through letting go.

The letting go can be very painful. When soul mates really need and want something from each other and they try to get it, sooner or later they realize they can't and they let go. That is a sad and painful day.

Usually they agree—the soul mates will agree, "Yes, I guess we have to let go." They usually both agree.

At that point, it's inevitable they will get back together. If they don't get back together, then they may be the kind of soul mates that part, that separate; but they always love each other no matter where the other one is. No matter whom the other one ends up meeting, the love does not end. They don't need to be together to feel the love.

Not every relationship is a soul mate relationship. But whether or not it's a soul mate relationship is something that stands to be revealed.

Now you may call it "twin flames" or the fervent search to find that magical opposite, but this has been going on on the Earth since human beings have been here. The term that's very popular these days is soul mate.

You have probably never heard of anything spoken or written by Yeshuwa (whom you call Jesus) on the subject of soul mates, have you? Or the Buddha on the subject of soul mates? Or any enlightened teacher or master. Why?

Did the masters forget something? Is it just something you invented in 1965? Hmmm?

Yes, relationships are important, vitally so. But if you go around looking for your other half, thinking something is missing until you find it, you will search for it until you die.

There are beautiful relationships, make no mistake. But better to see what the relationship has to offer and what it doesn't have to offer—than try to make it over into what you want. Better to learn from the fact that you are together—than to impose the reason about why you ought to be together, should be together, must be together, have to be together.

Discover what relationships show you. I promise you that those who lived their relationships out throughout their life—or even across several lives—did not sit down to discuss how their relationship was going, point by point. Ultimately, they did one thing: they gave up trying to make their partner into what they wanted. They just accepted: "She will be she, I will be I, and we are going to love each other." *They may not have wanted to do that!* They *had* to do that because love becomes the desire to have love. And peace becomes more important than agreement. And there is something vitally important about that.

What is important is that love must become increasingly unconditional and unlimited. It may start in an elegantly (or perhaps deceptively) insidious way that looks like everything has fallen into place. "We are perfect for each other." It's a trick! That's how the Creator— which is Love—gets Its foot in the door.

And after they get their foot in the door, many feel betrayed. They start seeing all kinds of things. The Creator says, "Ah—now they will have to learn about Love, not about agreement!"

You can seek agreement. But the funny thing about people who seek agreement in relationships is this: they tend to outgrow one another. "Well, we used to be in harmony but I'm no longer in that place. He won't grow! She won't grow!!"

This has little to do with a loving relationship. It may have to do with many other important and relevant things. But the thing that resembles something which one might call a *soul mate relationship* is *not* about agreement.

Yet those who truly love and accept each other (if they choose to and if they can find it) come to be in harmony with each other. They surrender to something greater than each of them. And that Love becomes the dictator, not the individual. That Love, not their personal desires, directs its own course.

A relationship doesn't get to be a soul mate relationship by your trying to make it one—or wondering whether it is or

not. It gets to be a soul mate relationship by just getting on with the business of seeking the spiritual experience, ceasing the fighting, and asking of the Spirit of the Universe, deep down within, "What would you have of me?" And then asking for the power to carry that out, daily. Sometimes it means asking many times each day. It's just as simple as that. No less simple than that and no more simple than that.

That simple thing is not so easy, but it's very simple. There are a lot of other things to do here and most of them are distractions. But if you can keep that simple kind of focus, "Creator, what would you have of me," and then seek the spiritual experience—inwardly in meditation or outwardly through signs—guidance comes. Guidance usually comes in both ways.

Requesting this is what prayer is. Seeking it means you are willing to serve that and put down the fight. Then you must ask for the power to carry out what is shown to you, because it will be shown to you in little ways, every day. And you will live a magical existence here, a very magical existence.

However, you will not be the programmer of your life. You will not be in control. The Spirit of the Universe will be in control. By the way, if you think you're in control now, it's a big delusion. It's just a matter of accepting that. That's all right.

Now that's another thing. There is a God. There is a Creator. And it is not you. You may be a co-creator, but the "co" is a very small part in that co-creating. A *vital* part of that co-creating, but a very *small* part. Your part is to seek guidance and get the power to carry it out.

It is very simple to understand why you are such a small part. It is not because you need to have a Creator like a big daddy or a big mommy in the sky because you are just a child and you have to listen (although that attitude can sometimes work). But it really isn't that.

It's more like this. Even though you're old souls here, and you know a great deal, and you have a great amount of experience, and you're of infinite capacity (in a sense), and all that sort of good stuff—how much do you really know of *All-That-Is?*

Whatever it is you think you know, you also know that *more* than what you know exists. In other words, there's that which you know that you know, and there's that which you know that you don't know. And if you think about it, that which you don't know is greater, by far, than that which you actually know. Isn't that so? But that's not all.

There is also that which you don't even know that you don't know— and that is greater by far than that which you know you don't know.

So we're starting with very little here.

You know something, but you know that you don't know a lot more than that. And you don't even know that you don't know what is far greater than that. So you actually know very little. And if you know very little, how can you function with a will as if you knew it all, except by creating lots of mistakes.

So why don't you just start with: "I don't know anything. Please show me." And when you seek deep down within, there is a place that is connected to everything. It doesn't take much humility to think, "All right, all right, I don't really know everything. What would you have of me? Show me."

The thing that allows you to do that is trust. If you've been hurt a lot and betrayed a lot and you don't have any more trust, even deep down within yourself, and you don't have any trust in God, or anything else, then it is all the more important for you to ask. Your faith and your trust in life will be restored through *spiritual experiences*.

Spiritual experiences restore trust. Your spiritual experiences will restore your trust. So ask for guidance and then seek within. Watch your inner screen of vision and your imagination and see what comes. If something doesn't come that way, then just be open in your life and you'll see little signs.

> TRUST

And what are these little signs? Is it a string of green lights when you didn't expect it? Yes! Is it that old lady or old man in front of you in your local store . . . the bill is a dollar ninety . . . only a dollar ninety . . . but he or she takes out a checkbook and begins to write a check. You're behind the person and you're frustrated because you're in a hurry. Yes, that's a sign! But it may not be just an obvious sign to slow down. You mutter, "Why is this happening to me?"

You know what that is? That's the appearance in your awareness of something other than your expectation; and it is revealing something to you. You're having a higher dimensional experience, right then and there.

These higher dimensional experiences occur all the time, but you will only notice them if you're looking, if you're asking, "Show me the way." If you're not asking "show me the way," you're not going to see a damn thing. But if you're asking, then you will start to see. You may not know what these experiences mean, but after a while you won't care. You'll say, "I don't care, there's another sign. I'm not alone."

Do you think I'm joking? I'm not! It gets just like that. You begin to realize you're not functioning in the universe alone. You're in harmony; you're in connection with a scheme of affairs that is very simple and very beautiful. And in your heart, constantly, there is a nearness to something that keeps opening doors to you and that's why you're here—for the expansion of love.

And where that will lead you, I promise, is beyond whatever agenda you could have created out of that which you *know*. Because there's all that which you know that you don't know and that which you don't even know that you don't know which is just waiting to be gifted to you so you can expand your experience, all the time.

I am not, in this moment, the only one telling you this. You will see messages of this kind everywhere. Everywhere! Through many venues. Why? Because it is truth and it comes because you need it; you have called out for help. You need your own communion with the Infinite, and it is very close to you. The guidance is everywhere, but you must seek it. You won't have to seek very far.

You see, that's openness. And you will need extraordinary openness. Extraordinary openness simply means *enough* openness to ask for help *one more time*. Help with what? Help with you! Help with the aspects of your own nature that you see—time and time again—create your own difficulties. You ask for help not so that you can get control over your life so you can theoretically enjoy it—but so you can be useful to the Supreme Love that is at work in the universe. So the Light of the Spirit may flow through you and you won't feel abandoned, cut off.

Those of you who think you can't feel, you can't see, you can't hear the Spirit world—even if you know it is there, even if you have felt it from time to time, even if you've had extraordinary spiritual experiences—

you just can't get woken up enough. And that's where it lies: In the self-examination and in the help of the Supreme. The help of the Supreme to help you with the parts of you that you trip over again and again—so that you can *be here, now*! And so that the Infinite "something" which exists as a resource within you can begin to flow.

So that is all that I will say for now. I shall go. Thank you for listening. We shall meet again.

✳

FOUR

THE TRUTH

Greetings to you, one and all. I am very happy and pleased to be able to join this wonderful group of seekers and finders into Truth.

The Truth is not something that I shall speak—or that you shall speak. The Truth is something other than that. *The Truth is a Living Spirit.* I don't mean a spirit like me or a spirit like you—although you are all reflections in some way of the Truth. What I mean is: Truth is *That-Which-Is*.

You are amongst the Truth even now. You are right now resonating with something, something that you are awakening to. And that which you are awakening to more and more is the reason why there are questions in your mind—about life, about your existence and what you are doing here—because there is a resonance about which you are growing more and more conscious.

This resonance does not club you on the head, and suddenly you have a potent spiritual awakening and, once and for all, you are in an ascendant reality, with all existence perfectly understood (although there has been a soul or two throughout time to whom this has happened).

And damn those souls!, I sometimes think. They cause so many problems for everyone else who does *not* evolve in that manner. We look for a light to become smashed upon our head or for some potent spiritual awakening that is the "Great It," after which you can pronounce yourself *God-Realized*—and create a following, of course.

But that is not how it happens. Or when it does happen like that, it is very rare. Besides, for those souls for whom that has happened, how do you know how many lifetimes they worked at that? The poor beloved Buddha, for example, suffered agonizing existences prior to the time of that great realization. As realizations go, by the way, that one happened fairly instantaneously—as realizations go. Yet even within that powerful spiritual awakening was the most intense kind of suffering you can imagine. The pain that drove the Buddha into the arms of the Creator was immense.

Some of you have also experienced some of that.

Now, because of so many awakening and awakened beings who have come into the world and who exist in the world now, you get to have the privilege of having learned enough so that some of your evolution can be gracious. *Some of your evolution!* I don't mean "some" in the sense that for some of you it can be gracious and for some of you it can't. I mean "some" as in: part of your existence may be a gracious and beautiful unfolding. And part of your existence may be rather torturous—from time to time.

The problem is that people often think pain means there is something is wrong. They think they are off of their path when they hurt.

And sometimes that is true. But the delusion is that if you were squarely on your path you would never hurt. I don't know what kind of path that would be; it sounds like a deluded path to me.

If you do not encounter any pain whatsoever, I think either there is a great deal of denial going on, or you have created a very elaborate fantasy. And one day that fantasy will be intruded upon by that which is greater than you.

In a way, many of us have lived in fantasy, and perhaps live in it to some extent right now—in a "reality" of our own creation. This is a very popular theme these days. I wonder why?

In this New Age (and I am *not* a "New-Ager" as I have told you before), the idea of "creating your own reality" is very popular. Human beings are

NEW AGE THINKING

coming into a sense of their own empowerment and connectedness to the universe and to the world. This is all integrating, and there is an enormous exhilaration at this time about the power to create the "reality" of your own choosing. Very interesting.

Yet I wonder how much you can really choose? And I wonder how much "reality" is getting created. Oh, I know *something* is getting created. But I wonder how much "reality" is getting created.

You can create whatever you are able to—whatever your abilities allow you to create—from whatever level of awareness and education and level of study can be inspired in you to create. But *toward what end?* What is the purpose of your creation (if you are indeed creating)? What is the motivation behind it? What are you trying to do?

You see, spiritually ascendant souls must reflect frequently about their motives. Frequently. Because there are a number of wounds that humans collect along their way, and what you may think is the creation of something very important to your spiritual development may be little more than simply trying to satisfy a few basic instincts—a few basic instincts for physical security or emotional security, or perhaps some sexual relations, or a place within your society.

And I will tell you something: While those things are important, they do not have much to do with your spiritual ascendancy. Learning how to negotiate your survival—because that is what I am talking about—is fundamental to your spiritual growth. But it is far from a sign that you are spiritually ascendant. And a lack of being able to negotiate these basic needs is not a telling sign of whether or not you are spiritually awakened. They are two separate things.

For example, this land of America where you live is a very independent land. There is a great deal of belief in personal responsibility. Self-reliance! I think that's a good idea. It's also a very competitive atmosphere. Survival of the fittest has been taken to all kinds of sophisticated heights that the American culture has labeled as "good."

For example, if you find yourself financially successful, you think you have understood the spiritual lessons of Life. Now that's odd. I can't seem to think of a single scripture in any religion that has ever spoken of how, if you are financially successful, you understand the keys to existence. Funny!

The same is true if you have a wonderful working relationship—or you don't, for that matter. Or finding your soul mate. If you think you have found your soul mate, some of you hold that up as a sign that you have understood the lessons of life.

But again, I can't find a single spiritual text ever written that talks about soul mates. Where is that found? Did all those enlightened souls forget something? Or did you invent something somewhere along the way that those unenlightened souls who came before you just totally overlooked? I wonder how much that has to do with—or doesn't have to do with—*anything*?

You are here for a business that is beyond your physical security and emotional security.

Now those securities cannot be denied; they are vital to your existence, that is certain. But frequently, the pursuit of these securities

YOU ARE HERE
TO WAKE UP

dominates one's life. And then where is there time for the whispering voice of the Spirit that speaks to your heart's nature, from which you gather your inspiration? How is there room for a voice that you can feel and attend to when you are desperate for those other concerns? So, yes, you must manage those needs; that is also part of your spiritual development. But it is very important to examine your motives.

What is it that is causing your struggle? What is it? How much of your life is consumed by things that are motivated by fundamental instinctual desires for survival? And how much is oriented toward your true spiritual inspiration? It is very important to *see* both of these things and to negotiate a balance between the two. Well, that may be much easier said than done. But that is the *business* of why you are here.

You are here to wake up to something—a truth that is resonating within your being, profoundly and accurately. But you must *seek* that!

Now many of you have been seeking that for some time and have been finding a little bit of it, more and more, here and there. And that is beautiful! That is beautiful.

It is not enough to have sought it once upon a time, twenty years ago. Or to have cultivated a spiritual or religious practice that you expect will "pay your dues" spiritually (so to speak) so that you can achieve a certain heightened state—especially if that practice has become rote in the process.

No, there must be a continuous conscious effort to contact that resonance, not an unconscious contact with it. And sometimes there are layers of things you must strip away so that you can allow yourself to feel that.

What do I mean by layers of things to strip away? Seek to *simplify* your existence—that is all that is involved in *stripping away*. Now to simplify your existence can mean a great number of things to each of you. But I am certain that within your awareness, you have some ideas about how to do that. Look at your complicated lives. All the time you can find yourself thinking: "Ah, I must get to this. I must make this a little less complex."

But if you have a number of desires plaguing you, or too many needs, they're going to distract you. That doesn't mean you need to throw away all of your desires, or disregard your needs. But I ask you: Do you have lots and lots of needs and desires? Are your needs and desires seemingly so relentless that they are torturing you? *Start with those*. Start with the ones that are the most intense and most plaguing, the ones that disturb you and cause you the most trouble—the ones that you constantly reach for that seem to elude you, no matter how hard you try.

| CULTIVATE |
| THE CONTACT |

It is there that *you need to ask for help*. It is there that the veils between the dimensions can be lifted. It is *there*—when you recognize that you are at the limit of what you are able to do and it has failed you—that you can then seek something beyond that.

Now in this land of self-reliance, many of you are not quitters. You will keep on trying and trying and trying. Trying to achieve whatever it is that is so important to you to achieve—no matter how many times you fail, no matter how much it hurts. And if you come to such a point where you are unable to achieve something, you will then brand yourself a failure, or "less than." Your self-esteem is attacked.

But what about those of you who stop, center yourselves, and ask: "Is there another way? Am I approaching what is *right for me*? Is there something else I need to be seeing?" Only the humble can ask such things. If you are filled with too much pride ("Oh, I can do it, no matter what—and I shall!") or your self-esteem is too low ("I am so lowly, I can never do that."), until that comes into *right size*, you can never ask.

So the heart must become humble and the mind must become open. And sometimes, those things can only happen after you have exhausted a great deal of all of what you believe you can do. But for those of you who are looking for a short cut to the reason why you are here, stop and ask, "Why? Show me. Give me a sign. Help me understand." Even though you do not know *what* is there listening, *if* anything is there listening, and you do not know how the response will come, *ask anyway*. And keep asking—all throughout your life. And you will become clearer and clearer.

You will begin to have a sense of *contact*. That contact, which first occurs as subtle intuitions, must be cultivated and refined as you go through life so that Spirit, which exists within you and around you, can come to clearly understand you—and so that you can come to clearly hear and understand the voice of Spirit.

Some of you may wonder why all of this is necessary. Well, even though this is a beautiful world that you are in, a magnificent world that you are in, you might have noticed that it isn't exactly the easiest place to be. Has anyone here noticed that? Now I have news for those of you who are sincere and take a great deal of personal responsibility: If you do happen to find perfect balance within yourself, the world will not suddenly become a perfect place (as some people tend to think). Some people think that if, inside, they are perfect, then the world they see will be perfect. Wrong!! This is not a perfect place! You will come, perhaps, to accept that *it is as it is*—and realize that you may not have an expansive enough vision to judge it as being beautiful, or bad, or whatever in between. But you will come to accept that *the world is the world*—and that you have a place in it.

| LEARN, GROW, LEAVE | But there is a business that you are here to do. To come and do your business, learn and grow, and *leave*. You see? Come and do your busi- |

ness. Learn and grow. And leave. You can't do everything that occurs to your mind, just because it is there to be done. You can't do it all.

Have you ever had a dream, for example, where you become very involved in the dream, for one reason or another? You create something, or do something, or involve yourself with something in that dream. It's a wonderful sort of thing. It's a very busy sort of dream. Or perhaps it's not wonderful, but you are getting something done. And then, all of a sudden—bamm!—you wake up. And you think: "I have to go back. I have to go back!" You may not even fully realize, right away, that you are awake. And you get very nervous. "I have to go back; I have to do it!" And perhaps you will try to complete your dream in your mind. But after a while you begin to wake: "Oh wait a minute. I can let go. It's just a dream. It's all right. I can let go!" Or perhaps there was a message in that dream for you which you then gleaned from the experience.

Have you ever had that experience? Have you felt that?

Well, *that* is what it is like, sometimes, at the moment of death. You create a number of involvements here in which you are very invested. And you may not always know which things are important and which are not. But those investments become very powerful at the time you are dying when you are leaving the body, and your relations come (and, believe me, they will come). And all of a sudden, you start reviewing your life.

Many people say that: "My life flashed before my eyes." That's right! But I tell you, for the person who is in that experience, it's no easy flash. It's a painful revelation for many. It may happen in a flash but you may become very concerned. "Did I do it right? Did I miss the point? Did I see it?"

There is a review, you see. It is for this reason that many who cross over—who speak about crossing over—talk about a judgment. Well, there is no judgment except as you are the judge. And, by whatsoever values you've created here, you'll judge yourself. So you'd better create some very loving values. I am serious about that! Some very forgiving values. Some very unconditionally accepting values because you are some terrible judges of yourselves at the time of death.

And there is an incredible urge to go back into the world at the time of death. A strong urge! That's why your relations appear and say, "Come.

YOU ARE
THE JUDGE

Come. We know. We know. Come. Come. Come." And they will try to urge you away. They will say, "Go. Go. Go!" And they will point you towards the Light. And you will think, "Well, all right."

You might say, "Isn't the Light compelling? I've read all these books. I've had some experiences. I've been told about the Light. And when that Light comes to me, I'm going to it! Because I've learned about that from those shows about life-after-death and so forth. And I know when that Light appears, I'm going. . . ."

But I'm not so certain. I've seen it over and over again. We watch. I've directed many. As a matter of fact, I will tell you something else. That doesn't *just* happen at the time of death. We are like that *right now*, saying: "All right. Come. Let go of some of those things now. We know you think they're important, but come." And we are calling you towards your destination. And we are saying, "Go. Now. Go towards the Light. You don't have to wait for death. Just go. Just keep going towards the Light." Those whispers of inspiration that come up: "It's all not as important as it seems. There are a few things to do here, that's true. But don't give it too much weight."

That's us speaking!

But it is very hard to convince you—because the very bodies that you are in are so dynamic. They magnify a very tiny portion of existence into such a powerful experience that it seems like reality to you.

| BODY AS MICROSCOPE |

It's like a scientist that looks through a microscope and sees a tiny little cell and becomes absorbed in the motion and activity of that cell. All these wonderful things are happening, and the scientist totally forgets that he is in a laboratory. And that outside of the laboratory is a building. And outside of the building is a city. And outside of that is more existence. And outside of that is a universe. And someone is saying, "Come. All right now, enough study of those cellular structures. Now come get into life here."

And that's what being in the body is like. The body is like a microscope that magnifies a tiny portion of existence *so that you can study it*, so that you can learn from it. But sometimes the larger context is entirely forgotten.

It is not enough to have heard the words of the enlightened ones, although that helps. You must have a *conscious contact* with the Source of existence, again and again. And you must seek direction from that contact. And the direction you must ultimately seek from that conscious contact is not: "All right, Creator, now that I've got a hold of you, how might I increase my income—because I really don't like the place where I live. And if I lived in a better place, couldn't I be a better servant?"

Well, I'll tell you, the Creator will accept that sort of "deal," sometimes in a peculiar sort of a fashion. But what about asking something like: "What would you have of me? What would you have of me because I don't know? I'm not certain again. Show me! How might I express Your Nature? How might I live in this nature that is truly my Self? How might I be an agency of that profound union which I have contacted?" Because therein lies the path.

There is a great deal that must be untangled. And it is often very difficult to disentangle what you have created lifetime after lifetime. It is almost impossible! In fact, the older a soul you become, the more complications you tend to create. And while you are coming back here to, theoretically, complete things and put things in order, you may create a few additional messes along the way—that you never intended to create. It becomes very complex, you see. And, without a complete memory of even one past life, how can you glean the perspective from your own mind, looking at the tiny little affairs you are involved in this time? How can you know? How can you set things right when you don't have the whole perspective?

That is why so many painful, difficult, and challenging things occur along the way. Because you are trying to set things in order when you don't have all the data. And sooner or later, you will discover that you don't have all the data.

The younger souls don't have the same problem. If they are sufficiently younger, it's a very simple thing. They say, "Listen, this is what I want. And this is what I am going to do." And they usually get it and do it. *This is enormously vexing to the old souls*. The old souls (I mean the old spiritual souls) look around themselves and say: "Wait a minute— I'm doing all this work on myself! I'm doing all of this growth. And why can't I stack up even a few little accomplishments, one on top of the other? Yet this one who is so *ignorant* of any spiritual reality— everything comes to him!"

OLD SOUL'S
DILEMMA

This is the greatest problem of old souls: *envy* of the younger souls who seem to get everything so easily. The old souls think: "Wait a minute. God (if there is one, dammit!) hates me! There's something wrong here!" Now it isn't really that way, but this is how they feel: "Why does everything I do, not work!? Even the simplest things I try to do seem to work out almost the *opposite* of how I intend."

Has anyone here had that experience? Yes? You are the old souls!

You do not know how many complicated karmas you are working against. You are not aware of the context in which you function. It's not: "I do this, and this happens." In fact, by the time you set anything in motion, the opposite happens. It is too complicated! *You cannot sort it out that way!* If you don't believe me, just keep trying. Find out for yourself. It doesn't work! It doesn't work. Not for the older soul.

The older the soul gets, the closer they *must* get to: "Thy will be done." Because anything else just doesn't work out right. Not for the older soul.

This is an enormously difficult point to get across, especially in America, a land that is very self-reliant, and especially where the spirituality that is evolving here is in keeping with such self-reliant beliefs.

Now, every land creates a spirituality that reflects the culture of that land. In this one, it is: "The more spiritual I am, the more I get what I want." That is essentially the way spiritual belief manifests in this land. And the "belief" isn't any truer in any other land. They just have their own version in their own cultural context. But in this land, "spiritual means more and better" tends to fit the cultural context. So, somehow or another, you must get beyond the cultural context.

The first thing that tends to happen when an older soul begins to get this message from the spirit world—which is, "My friend, it doesn't work like that," is that the older soul becomes angry and sad. They begin to get little hints all around them and think, "What are you saying, Universe? Are you saying I can't have what I want? Is that what you're saying? Are you saying that what I want isn't possible? Is *that* what you're saying? Because if *that* is what you are saying, then I don't want to hear it! I don't want to know that! I don't want to believe that! It can't be as horrible as that! Oh, why am I here? I want to die!"

That's another common feeling of the old soul and it is the beginning of a very powerful spiritual awakening.

Now many old souls have been here so many times as old souls that they think they remember something from some other lifetime, like: "Wait a minute. I know I've gotten distracted a number of times." So that when they hear some of the messages of the enlightened and read some of the things that the enlightened have written, they say: "Yes, yes. This all makes sense. I remember something about distraction. I know how vulnerable I am to all of this confusion. I'm going to devote myself to a spiritual life because I remember something of this." Or "I'm going to lock myself away in a monastery."

Well, frequently that doesn't work either, you see. Because the motivation behind that is not fully awakened (except for a few who really are ready and, even then, this may not necessarily be the highest path for them). For most, the motivation behind this kind of thinking is often about hiding from the very pain I've just been discussing—the pain that comes when a soul thinks: "Wait! What are you saying? I can't have what I want? This is a life of suffering?" And so, you see, sometimes that soul is going into those circumstances (into a monastery, for example) in order to protect themselves from their fear of suffering—their memory of suffering. They don't want to suffer again.

| MOTIVES MATTER | It cannot be a motivation like that. Eventually that motivation, too, must evolve. All the *fear* as well as the *fighting* must eventually be laid down. Because |

deep down within is where the doorway to the Supreme Love is found. And so long as you are fighting, for any reason, no matter how valid, you can't find the doorway.

Sooner or later, you must grow tired of the fight, or decide the fight isn't for you. Or else you must go out and experiment and prove that you can do exactly what you want and have exactly what you want. And if you are "good," then you may achieve it! I don't mean a "good person." I mean *clever*. I mean *powerful*. If you are skillful, powerful, clever, and can articulate and express all the devices you have learned in all of your lifetimes, then you may be able to do it. But you may find that others who are more talented than you, who have achieved it in that way (or who have tried and have not achieved it in that way), may be missing something.

Now there are those who have gleaned some of the external things that perhaps some of you want; and maybe they came about it by a different grace. But those who came to it by manipulating and power driving—without their spirituality—have found at the end of that road they still feel empty; and they wonder why.

But those who have found it while holding their spirituality realize that "something" has helped them, every step along the way. And that's a different deal.

But usually if you haven't proven to yourself that it doesn't work like that, you may need to try to prove that you can do it that other way. And what you may accumulate—if you're clever—is a few, simple, little instinctual needs. A little financial security, some material security, some physical security. A little emotional security. You see? You may have a partner or two. Some amount of sexual relation in your life—if you're young enough to still care about such things. And a place in your society.

And it doesn't really mean all that much.

If you are an old soul, I have news for you: *You've done that already!* And do you know how you know that you've done that already? Because as soon as you get on board to start to achieve those things— things which have become very important to you—suddenly you don't have the energy to do it. "Oh, I can't stand this school anymore. Why am I here?" Or as you are going up the ladder of your success, you are saying: "Well, I'm getting the money—but I want to run for the hills! This isn't worth it!" And as you are going after that, all the while you are asking yourself: "Why am I doing this?" You see, it's that memory in the back of your mind: "I did this already!" And most of you can't find the enthusiasm.

So some of you take a few "You Can Do It!" seminars that help you to power yourself to continue, no matter what you feel. And you come out of those seminars filled with energy and light; you grab a hold of those metaphysical tools that support your intention, and you drive yourself! And a week later, a month later, you're back where you started again. There's no power! You don't have the power. The power that you don't have is your dilemma. The truth is: *You don't have the power*.

POWER

You are a speck in existence. Power comes from something other than your will. True power is not within your will. A limited amount of power is within your will. And the power that is within your will is a very simple kind of power, given to you by the Source of existence—for survival. You can muster whatever you have to do to survive. Beyond that, if your will can achieve a few things for you, so be it. But you may feel a bit exhausted by that, if you're an old soul.

An old soul needs an *Infinite* power—power beyond the power of their own will. Old souls have been exhausting their will, life after life after life. And they just can't do it anymore. The lack of power is their dilemma. An old soul needs the Infinite to rely upon.

Now the younger souls—or the unenlightened souls—tend to think that this is weakness. But it is the way of strength. Connection to the Infinite *is* the way of power. And that connection to the Infinite (I'm not talking about the will), that connection to the Infinite is without limit. And it cannot be used in just any old fashion.

If you are of the mind to be seeking that power, and if you are seeking why you are here, then gradually you will have an awakening, day by day by day. Occurrences within and around you will create an awakening. And you will experience this gradual awakening most days of your life.

But what you will *not* experience is "my will be done!" If you are an old soul, you'll have a great and difficult time with "my will be done." Because you don't have it anymore! *You've spent it.* You need more than that, much more than simply "my will be done." You need to have a spiritual awakening. So you must *seek the spiritual experience.* If you are an old soul, you *must* seek the spiritual experience.

Understanding the talks, the lectures, the books, the scriptures, the texts, the teachers—is not enough. *Experience is what you need.*

SEEK SPIRITUAL
EXPERIENCE

You must seek the spiritual experience. Meditation and prayer is where you find the spiritual experience, first. And then the veil between the dimensions begins to lift, and you lose the ability to separate the inner from the outer. The illusion that there is a separation between the inner and the outer gradually disappears. And then the spiritual experience starts happening, not only within you as inspiration, but it seems to start happening around you as well—little miracles, little synchronistic events. You have entered into another dimension of existence.

What is that dimension of experience? Well! You took your eyes out of the microscope! And now you're in the *real* world. You're no longer looking through the microscope.

Every now and then, you may have to check into that microscope for little "reality checks," so to speak. Every now and then, you must contend with the instinctual drives and with your world. But without your contact of meditation and prayer, from which spiritual experience comes, you cannot find the feeling that will guide you. But once you begin to find some of that feeling that guides you, then you can get a response when you ask: "Show me."

Where *we* come in is very simple. We are your Spirit Guides and

Teachers. People become enormously excited when we start appearing in their lives. We start talking to them in their heads, or they find themselves slipping into trance states, or they find themselves out of the body and we start coming through them. Or they hear of us through channels and psychics and mediums. They start having some psychic experiences, and they get very excited. It all becomes very stimulating.

However, they become very disappointed when they find out that *we have very little power to do anything for them*. We're just guides. We can't make you do what we think is right. That's not even what we want to do. And we cannot keep you from what we think is wrong— although sometimes we would like to do that. But when we try, oftentimes we overstep our bounds. And you resent it. You call us "manipulative" and all sorts of things. So we often have to pull back: "All right, do what you want!"

Yes, we have very little power to do either of those things. Our power, our great power, comes in this way: When you seek the Source of existence and Its direction for you, whatever you then receive as inspiration and you try to do what you feel that the Supreme Love would have you do (as a result of seeking that contact—not just because you made it up but because you *sought* the contact). When you try to do what you feel is right based upon that, *that's* where our power comes in.

Whatever choices you then make, we are given to help that turn round right. (And I say that only because you may have "got" the thing wrong . . . .) Doesn't matter! That's where our tremendous power comes in. Then it doesn't matter what you do; it doesn't matter what the deal is.

If you seek the Creator and do what you sincerely feel is right as a result of that contact, then we are given the power to help that turn out in some way that greatly benefits you. Most things in life tend to happen rather automatically. And if you are in the habit of seeking guidance when you are facing indecision, if you're in the habit of seeking guidance: "What would this Love have of me?" then we can be powerful. We have great power.

Now, asking this question doesn't mean a damned thing if you haven't sought a conscious contact with your Creator. Because when you say, "What would you have of me?" and you've never sought a conscious contact, you won't *feel* a thing. Oh, maybe some inspiration, some unwitting motive will surface. We can still help you with that, by the way; and we usually will. But it doesn't happen powerfully until you seek a *conscious* contact, and then practice refining that conscious contact so that we can clearly understand you. And so that *you can* clearly understand the Spirit.

Cultivate a conscious contact. Develop it. Seek the Higher Will for you. It is inclusive of you, believe

| CULTIVATE CONSCIOUS CONTACT |

me. When you think, "Creator, show me. What is Your will for me?" the Creator does not say, "Aahh, now let me find something for this one that benefits everybody else *except* this one." It doesn't work like that. But sometimes, that's what people feel when they approach that guidance. They think, "Well, what if it's something where I'm always helping somebody else?"

Well, so what? So what if you have to help someone else now and then. Who knows what you might be setting right—that you can't remember. Other people with whom you have had incomplete relationships may be back in your life because you need to get back into that old "dream" and finish that business. And so they're in your life. And maybe you can help them once in a while, without their giving anything back in return. Maybe that will help you too in some way.

But usually, what happens when you seek guidance is that you keep yourself out of the trouble you might have created had you *not* sought guidance when you faced indecision. Because usually, when you face indecision and come up with what you feel is a powerful decision after you've been indecisive for a very long time, it's usually urgency that is motivating you. And usually, you are about to do something wrong, something that may not turn out well.

So better that you at least seek your inner, deeper nature, even if some unconscious motivation does try to misguide you. Because if you do that, we will help!

And that is not only our *promise* to you, that is our dictate. That is our love. That is our passion. That is why we exist! There is no other reason for our existence, save to reach to those souls who are still suffering—so we can help them, if their focus is on the Source. Elsewise, there's just too much confusion and we can't get through it.

So focus on the Source and ask for guidance, and you will see the signs of our assistance and the signs of the Infinite Presence with you.

✳

FIVE

THE PATH OF THE OLD SOUL

I have a question for you. What are the things you endure which, when exposed to them, make you grow? And here's another question: What is your purpose? What is the purpose for living here in this world, *now*?

Many of you have come across a spiritual reality. You have had various and sundry spiritual experiences. And as a result of those, you have had some degree of awakening. For a moment, you have glimpsed a truer self, a truer being, a higher self, a more important reality, an empowered stated of mind and spirit—only from time to time to lose sight of that glimmering place. Why? And what is the purpose of that? Are you to live without it? Or is the point to live in that state of glimmering being, permanently? Is that why you have come here?

Well, I have an answer for you. To put it simply, all you come here to do is to make progress. That's all. To make progress. To learn, to love, to awaken. And to experience life and consciousness for the gifts that they are.

It's up to you to find where the gift in it is. It's up to you to experience that. It is truly up to you. And if you do not find it (and it only comes as a result of seeking it), then you will not know.

The Gift

But if you seek it, you will find it; and then you will find more of it. And then, more. And a higher world, another dimension, will become more visible. And that other dimension has many, many things associated with it that are very beautiful. Some of those things you will never understand. Never. Some of those things will be beyond your wildest imagination. Your wildest imagination! What do I mean by that? Just this: There is nothing here which anybody can conceive of which is greater than anything that will be revealed to you. There is nothing here that you can imagine that is so far fetched it is not included in the ultimate reality of things. For the ill or the good. These are things which are far greater than your understanding. And to be able to touch such a reality and hold it will not happen if all you will do is work towards instinctual survival.

You cannot find it that way. You must look beyond your survival instincts. You must recognize what those instincts are and realize there is more. And just because you realize that does not mean you'll hold on to it. It does not mean that you won't forget, you see.

Just before we came here today, we heard Mataare say something about how it "all goes back." Yes, that is true, whatever it is, all goes back. But it is also true that all is given. So you don't have to worry about either. It all goes back and there is always more given. Perhaps it is better to say that it is all borrowed—so appreciate it while you have it, while you are here. You all have something right now that is very valuable. Look around and you will see it. Look inside and you will feel it. But you must look for it or you will not see it or feel it.

And unless you find it, this spiritual dimension that allows you to appreciate life, all you will feel is your pain and your suffering.

And do you know what that pain and suffering is for old souls like yourselves? Jealousy and envy. Jealousy and envy. They are the bane of the old soul. Do you know what envy sounds like? "Why do other people have all that? What have they done to deserve it? I have been doing all of this work. Where is mine?" That is envy.

Jealousy? Jealousy is wanting what you do not have. Or wanting to keep what you are afraid you will lose. Envy and jealousy. The bane of the spiritual being.

Jealousy and envy are like a virus, a disease, a sickness. Neither is evil. Neither is not good. They are both a sickness. And where does this sickness come from? The source of each, believe it or not, is your own self-hatred.

When you are in the experience of jealousy or envy, you are in the experience of self-pity, of self-loathing. "Why them and not me?" In

> JEALOUSY
> AND ENVY

essence, you are saying: "I'm not worth it." And many times you think that is a direct message from God that says: "You're not worth it."

And then you go into re-play: "What do you mean by that, God? Are you really saying I am not worth it? Is that what you are trying to say? Is that why I am so deprived, and why they can have and I can't? What am I? A nothing?" You see?

Envy and jealousy are symptoms of your own un-love, your own un-like for yourself. It has nothing to do with God. It has to do with the fact that you have not yet found what you love about yourself. You have not yet found the real meaning of unconditional love, starting with yourself!

<table>
<tr><td>UNCONDITIONAL LOVE</td></tr>
</table>

Now perhaps at some point you have received some unconditional love, by some gift, that you were able to experience from another towards you. And that helped you in loving yourself. Your being was validated simply because you existed. Someone loved you.

Maybe when you were younger, one day you were simply told, "Oh, I just love you so much just because you are you. I don't care what you become or don't become, what you own or don't own, what you prove or don't prove, how smart you are or how dumb. I don't care if you are pretty or not pretty, handsome or not that attractive. I don't care. I just am glad you exist. Come here. I love you (kiss!)." You see?

But maybe you never received that. Maybe when you heard "I love you", it was really saying: "I will love you more when you do better in school—because I really don't like you that much when you don't do well." Maybe you also heard, "I'll punish you if you don't start doing better." Or maybe you heard, "I love you as you are, so beautiful—but I like your hair with a bit more curl. Or I like you better when you are wearing those clothes or when you don't tear them." "Or I approve of you more when you listen to me." You see? Maybe you heard things that were supposed to speak to one part of you—but your mind, young or old, understood it another way.

And maybe that made you decide to get your needs taken care of this way or that so you could get your need for acknowledgment addressed. And maybe you thought that was love. And if you're an old soul and bought that, sooner or later you will rebel against it and say something like this: "I'm not going to do anything!"

When they are young, old souls are astonishing achievers and manipulators. They know how to get just what they want. And they are willing to pay almost any price for it. Maybe they will excel at school. They will follow everything that they are told to do; they will even do something very winning. Then, in the next moment, they say, "Forget it!" and do the opposite—in every respect.

Suddenly these overachievers and manipulators can't hold a job. Suddenly, they can't do anything. They do a complete 180; they go in the opposite direction. And then, when they take a moment and look at themselves, they once again feel their lack of self-love and conclude, "I am worthless. I can't do anything. I am so dysfunctional. I can't work. I can't do the things that other people do."

Ah, these old souls! They will find little ways to skinny through every unfortunate circumstance and take advantage of every opportunity. They will manipulate. They will make things happen for themselves. And when they take on a new lover, they take on a hostage. That's right, old souls do not take on new lovers. They take hostages.

They will draw people in and then clobber them with something like: "You better serve me! You better be exactly what I want you to be! If you don't, if you aren't, then we will have to have one of those discussions." Ahh, it's all arranged, you see.

TAKING HOSTAGES

But sooner or later, it all just stops working for the old soul. The older the soul, the less it works. They either give up relationships altogether—or they find someone that has taken them hostage while they think they are taking the other one hostage. You see! And sooner or later this tension builds and builds, and if they haven't already given up on their partner, they will say something like this: "All of womankind is terrible. All of mankind is awful. I'll take no one. Just give me a servant and a lover now and then—and perhaps some money! But I'm not going to saddle myself with any permanent partnership of any kind. No, I am not!"

The older souls tend to do that. They are tired. Their spirits are very tired, quite often. And often if they are in a relationship, it can look to an outside party that one is being done great favors by the other. A little symptom of hostage taking.

SUCCESS OF
NEWER SOULS

Old souls are very interesting. I can tell an old soul, but I can't tell them anything! Old souls are the last ones to listen. That is how I was. I have some reputation for how much I didn't listen through out my incarnations. The old souls must have some experience of doing everything wrong, once, at least. And sometimes many times. And this is very confusing for old souls. The reason why it is confusing for old souls is because old souls tend to look at some of the newer souls and they don't know they are newer souls.

An old soul may make the mistake of thinking that newer souls are actually old ones because they get things done. They seem in control of their lives. They are happy! They have social position, a fine mate, a good income, and nice things. Old souls deduce that since those people know how to succeed, since they are good at getting the life they want, that must mean they are old souls.

But they are wrong. That success is almost always a mark of a new soul: whether they follow the beaten path or not, new souls get things done—with a power and a vengeance and a will. The reason they can do that is because they are newer at it. They are full of inspiration, vigor, vim, energy, life, enthusiasm, and positivity.

Old souls can be astoundingly negative. New souls rarely have to make any kind of positive affirmations because they are full of will and positivity. They cannot understand why all those old souls are sitting in a room chanting over and over, "I deserve prosperity. I deserve love . . . ."

You would think that after all of these incarnations an old soul would know this. They have lived through all of the pain many, many incarnations, over and over again. And they know somewhere in a faint memory that it is not supposed to be such a struggle. They remember the days they were powerful as king this and queen that. They remember being "somebody" and that "somebody" was rich, famous, powerful. They remember the potency they once had.

Old souls are not the same as new souls. Old souls have a job to do. And I will not lie to you: that job is not an easy job. There is nothing easy about it. If you think it is easy, you haven't been around long enough.

Oh it can be fulfilling and it can be rewarding. But it isn't easy. You struggle with your psyche. You struggle with your ego—or your lack of ego! You see the world open to younger souls; they can do anything. But you—you have already done everything and that is why you say: "I can't do that, I can't do this. I can't do it this way. I can't be here. This isn't right! I won't get married. I won't stay married. I won't do this. I won't do that!"

Old souls are very hard to please. Why? Because they have done it all already and they don't want to go through it again.

Old souls have left the most difficult things to do for last. And that is why it is not easy. That is why old souls struggle. The Creator doesn't have it in for you. Old souls have done all the other business but the business they do not want to do. So when the time comes for them to do that, it isn't easy.

This is the dilemma of the old soul. And the first thing an old soul must learn is that the power of their will is not infinite. So long as an old soul thinks, "I am unlimited, I am God," he or she is going to have a big problem. Old souls will have a huge craving. That is why you will hear them telling themselves how unlimited and infinite they are. You hear them chanting incredibly confused things like: "You can have it all."

Well, who needs it all? Who wants it all? Anyone who says that is an incredibly confused soul. And that "anyone" is usually the old soul, well on her or his way to developing an insatiable appetite that can never be satisfied. Nothing will ever be enough, not even a belief that "I am God. I am unlimited."

The fact that nothing is enough is tied directly to an old soul's underlying fundamental negative belief: "I am not enough. I am not good enough. I am nothing."

New souls don't think like that. They don't even query, "Can I have it all or can't I have it all?" They just do what they have to do. You will often hear them say things so callous to old souls as, "Oh just get it done. Stop talking philosophy and just do the job. Just do it. Wake up. Get on with it. Snap out of it. Get over it!"

And the old soul replies, "But I can't. I'm trying but I can't. I am not enough. I'm not God." Aaah, it's time for that old soul to connect to the Infinite Source. That is the next step and it is the only solution. There is no other. An old soul disconnected from the Infinite Resource is miserable.

Sooner or later that old soul contacts that pain, profound and unquenchable. And that pain is their teacher and their salvation. And it will always be so.

But what is this pain? Well, first of all, old souls realize that they must stop looking for the quick fix, for the easy way out—the fast way to make the money, the best relationship there is, with the most perfect person there is.

They also begin to realize that other souls, often younger souls, possess so much more because they have worked for it! And the old soul doesn't want to hear about that, about hard work; they don't want to be one of those worker bees. They want it all to be the easy way; they have been here too long for any of that.

But the reverse is actually true: the older soul must be humble enough to become a worker bee if that's what it takes. Sometimes the beginning of older souls loving themselves is about doing just like the younger souls do—they feel good, on some level of feeling, about what they are able to do.

An older soul must sometimes set up a series of smaller successes for themselves so they can have a good feeling about being

No Quick Fix

successful. About small things. This is very important. Yes, the old soul must set up small ways to be successful. A little at a time. a little at a time regarding their health. A small success regarding their spirituality. A small success about their self-worth. The old soul must stop grander dreams. Grander dreams are not for the old soul. Grander dreams are for younger souls.

The old soul will never achieve a grand dream by going after a grand dream. Why? Because old souls already think they have a right to it! And when a little faltering happens on the way to some grand dream, they get so depressed that they end up saying it's not worth anything anyway. You see?

So the old soul must become humble enough—open enough—to see a smaller distance. Old souls must be self-reflective and look at themselves and say, "Where oh where throughout my life has all my manipulating left me? Despite my sincerity, despite my earnest soul searching, where has all this manipulating left me? It's left me with a weak character! Maybe it's time for me to develop my character."

They will need to look upon themselves daily and think, "Could I have done somewhat better today?"

"And if I should be a little better, where do I get the power for this because today I did all I could. Where do I get what I need to do more?"

But if you are an old soul, you may not know how to get any better. In fact, that is certainly almost always so: You don't know how to do any better. You don't have the power to do so! And maybe that is what spirituality is all about for an old soul—seeking the Source in order to get the power you need without having to do more than you have the power to do. To be a little more loving towards yourself, for example, than you otherwise had the power to be. And then appreciate yourself a little more than you formerly had the power to do.

| SEEK THE POWER | You see, the old soul must seek that power from the Source of existence. And that Source will always be found deep within your innermost nature. |

What does *seeking the power* mean? It means you must pray. Prayer is the way the soul gets around the ego and connects to the higher self. Through prayer you relinquish the emotions in favor of conscious contact. Prayer doesn't invalidate those emotions; it simply puts you in touch with what is on the other side of them—the truth of who you are.

It means you must meditate. It means you realize that you cannot simply ride this out. You have to become deeply devoted to your path. All old souls do this. In some period in their life, they become deeply devoted to some spiritual or religious path. Inevitably! And then, they go back to sleep and float.

They can float for years. Sometimes for decades! And they forget what got them there. They forget about all that praying they had done, all that devotion they had dedicated, all that meditation they had sought. They forget they did all of those things. They forget that that was why they were in the higher dimension for a while.

Instead, they thought they could just hide out in those religious or spiritual paths. They thought they had it made, you see, at that time. And then they get disappointed—so disappointed—when they inevitably see flaws in that path or that teacher. And they feel betrayed, these old souls. But they were never betrayed. They just did not know the truth from the false. They did not see clearly then; and they may not be seeing clearly now.

The message of the Truth is always the same: Deep down within your innermost nature lies the doorway to the Source of all power and the Father of Light, and the Mother of Light. Deep down within your innermost nature. And you must seek that power and exercise it in the Light that you have found there—and do a little more good.

That is the doorway to the higher dimension. When you get that and accept that, as a result of your experience you will know all about that other world.

As human beings, there is so much that needs to be understood. It is sometimes so difficult for human beings to recognize the connection between the sciences and the spiritual. To many people— to religionists, spiritualists, and scientists alike—they seem a world apart. But not to the old soul.

The old souls (whether scientist, spiritualist, religionist, or anything else) have always felt the connection but they could never exactly prove it or totally identify the missing link. They can't quite do that. They try but they can't quite connect it.

But there is a connection.

And when you go deeply into your innermost nature, where exactly do you go? Those of you who have met consciousness there (your own and otherwise—and it is sometimes hard to differentiate which is what because at some point we are one). For those of you who have met consciousness there, tell me: What are you meeting and where are you meeting what you are meeting? What is that all about?

When as a child you looked up at the heavens and the stars, why did you think you had to go there? Why did you think *God is there* before you were even told there was a God? Why did you feel compelled to go there when you looked at the moon and the stars and the sky? Why?

Because gravity held you to the earth and you felt frustrated? Why are you so compelled? Even though you cannot go there with your bodies, you feel compelled there? Why do you feel so free when you finally contact some spiritual experience that calls you to feel your unlimited Self? Well, maybe you knew that you are everywhere—just as well here as there. Just as well there as here. Why do you feel that? Free? What state is that? What dimension is that?

When you travel through space—so-called physical space—far enough and long enough, why does time distort? Why does the relationship between space and time become so hard to understand that at some point it is entirely indistinguishable?

Is there a relationship between when you are having a spiritual experience and when and why space and time become entirely indistinguishable? What is your connection with All-That-Is? And why is it said that heaven, so to speak, is in the sky or up there—and likewise here as well, at least to some degree? Is there a relationship? What kind of beings are you—really?

And how much of that is understood or even tasted when you simply try to survive from one day to the next? How will you ever ponder these things?

How will you ever discover about those kinds of things? How will you get anywhere? How will you find out the Truth? How will you, unless you make time for it? Unless you make time for the Truth?

The little reliefs you have from time to time are not enough. Having finally found a partner, for example, after

RELIEF IS NOT ENOUGH

searching for so long may be an incredible relief for a short time. But has that ever been the answer when, before you know it, you find out that you and your partner have issues. You wanted so desperately for finding a partner to be the answer. But it could not be. It could only be a tremendous, a beautiful relief—a relief to an instinctual search. But then you found that you needed more than mere relief.

Now for some, this becomes very terrible because they do not realize that they need more—more than the instinctual relief of companionship. So they keep looking for that companionship to be something that it can never be. And that is very painful.

For some old souls, this can be so painful and constant that they keep coming and going from relationship to relationship, looking for just that right one, thinking that the relief they will one day find will be the answer to their life. And even then, if they are an old soul, they will say, "No, no, I know that is not the answer to my life. I know it." And yet they keep on looking for instinctual relief.

Why? Because that is what those old souls are hoping for—they are hoping for an answer and they are thinking, "Why not this? Why not me?" But there is so much more than that. So much more.

The same is true with work and money. And even with your physical well-being and your security and your place in society amongst your peers. All those things are just the animal in you trying to provide for its instinctual survival. And we know you must seek this, as individuals and collectively as a species.

We know that you want to have a place amongst your peers, you want some acknowledgment, some recognition. You want the body who looks at you to say, "Yes, you are worth something." That is not just your ego. That is your species! That is a speciel instinct. Your species cannot survive unless it is societal. If you do not have intraspeciel relationships, no individuals will make it by themselves. Every species must have a culture to live amidst so the species can have some longevity. So when you want some recognition, that is a speciel instinct. But it is not a great spiritual gold mine; it is simply your instinct to survive as a species.

When you want a lover or when you want to have sex, that is also a speciel instinct. That's built into you. When you want to have job security and you want that house or that piece of land, all those things are instincts so you can feel safe in your person. That is an instinct you have as an animal for safety. The fulfillment of speciel instincts and animal instincts is a relief but it is not spirituality.

It is compensation—but it can never fill your soul. Security won't fill your soul. Relationship won't fill your soul. Recognition cannot address your soul. The satisfaction you legitimately feel in those things does relieve your instincts. But the two—instinct and spirituality—are not the same. Each one is vital but they are different.

Now the old soul is a very good instinct reliever. But in some instances, you will still hear this: "Well, if I am supposedly such a good instinct reliever, why haven't I accumulated the things that my instincts demand? I may get 'stuff' but I don't really feel all that relieved."

That's because, somewhere along the line, you as an old soul did not realize that fulfilling those instincts was not the same as fulfilling your soul. And because you did not realize that, you kept seeking fulfillment as an instinctual beast. And it was never enough to relieve your soul. As a result, you began to collect instinctual relief impulsively and compulsively until you had accumulated so much in this life (or in others) that you were in agonizing pain for not having your soul relieved. And so now you resent the fact that you have to do *anything* to address your instincts. And so you refuse to!

Many of you have lived as monks, nuns, and renunciates because of this, because you so resented the memory of previous incarnations where you accumulated all those things and yet felt so betrayed. You felt so betrayed that you decided you would never put yourself through that again! "Because, God damn it, that's not why I am here."

And that is why you can't stand to see anybody else working hard and getting ahead. Because you refuse to do that anymore. And that puts you in a bad position as a spiritual being and as an old soul. You see?

For an old soul, the spiritual experience is the last house on the block. And yet there is nowhere else they can go. They must go directly to the Source of Existence for all their answers. And even though old souls may know this, they really don't do this. Even though they believe this, they also don't do that simple thing. The old soul often mistakes belief in their previous experience of God for faith. But they have no faith.

Many, many old souls have no faith. And they certainly don't have any trust.

They have experienced something, but they do not trust what they have experienced. They are the skeptics. Old souls look askance at just about everything; they are looking for the flaw. They have a very negative eye but see themselves as wise.

They can see the hole, the flaw, in just about everything—and, as a result, think they are smarter than everyone else. "I can't believe how naïve everyone else is," they say.

But those same souls are often not aware of how desperate they themselves are. While they count everyone else naïve, someone comes along and relieves them of an instinctual pain—and those old souls give that person everything in return. So deep is their pain that they cannot help but be naïve, gullible, and vulnerable themselves.

What to do? What to do?

Old souls must accept their condition. They must fall on their face, sometimes often, before their understanding of God and the universe and allow themselves to say: "Help! Help! I am helpless here. Without *You* I am nothing, God. Only You can save me from this world. Only *You*, Divine Source. Only *You*. Only *You*!"

And they ask: "What would You have me do? What would You have me do? What would You have of me? "

Then finally an intimacy develops between the old soul and the Divine. And that is where the trust develops and the resentment at life begins to end. You see? That is when the other dimensions begin to open visibly, and more consistently. That is when the old soul begins to be surprised over and over again at just how fast and miraculous the truth of life really is. They see that it is greater than they ever imagined. Beyond their wildest dreams. And believe me, it gets very wild.

Many of you, when you opened up spiritually and asked, never expected you would run across things called "Guides." Guides

SURRENDER

may not have been something you ever heard about. You probably never thought you would be pulled into strange circumstances, with even stranger beings. Maybe you never thought any of this would happen. Maybe all you thought was that you might get a little relief and a little beauty and a little love from following what seemed to you to be your simple spiritual path.

You never thought the whole world would open to you. You never thought you would have to surrender. You probably never really knew what *surrender* was.

Maybe you did not realize that surrender meant you were going to have accept what-is. Maybe you thought surrender meant something you read about or were told about by the latest saint or master on the block. You never thought.

You never thought that surrender might mean when the bill came in and the money was not enough to meet it—that surrender might mean simply, "Oh, I have to let go. Oh, what would you have me do?" You never thought it might mean that, would mean that, does mean that.

You thought it meant that if one day you were standing at the foot of a great mountain and the herds that were following you could not pass, that surrender would mean, "My God, move this mountain!" And that if your surrender was sufficient, the mountain would part and the herd that was following you would be let through. That is what you thought surrender would mean.

You did not know surrender would mean that you would have to go into work one more day when you really didn't want to. You never thought surrender would mean that.

You never thought it would mean that you might have to extend a little more patience to your lover or your partner. Or a little bit more to yourself if you are alone. You never thought that surrender would mean that.

Perhaps you thought it would mean that if only you were to meditate and focus long enough, you could finally let go of some inner stress and suddenly your being would be full of Light. You thought surrender would be like that. You never knew it meant that when your knee is creaking and your back is hurting because you have been sitting all of ten minutes, that surrender might mean sitting another three minutes to see if you can just hang on a little longer.

You might have thought that surrender meant that if Jesus Christ came and everybody else thought he was some rastafarian maniac, you would see clear through his eyes and say "This is the Lord of All"—because you were so surrendered that you would have the right eyes to see—or something like that.

You never thought that surrender might mean that, after your religion turned you off, you would still remember prayer. You never thought it might mean that the higher dimension is still here with you now.

Surrender might mean letting go of your pain, letting go of your resentment sufficiently to commune with the Spirit of the universe deep down within your innermost nature. And where is that Spirit of the universe? It occurs when you get soulful. What happens when you go into your pain? Well, yes, it does hurt. But very soon it isn't the world anymore. Soon it isn't the event or the person. It is a sadness with yourself and the whole world disappears. And it leaves you with what? You see.

Deep within your innermost nature. And you didn't have to even meditate. There you are, with yourself. Perhaps this is a moment for your humble communion with the innermost Divine. Why not? You are already within yourself. Why not, then, a time for meditation, prayer, communion with the inner Divine? Maybe your pain is a gift to the doorway of the Infinite.

That is why we wouldn't take away your pain. We wouldn't take it away if we could. We are Guides, you see; we are not fortune tellers. Oh, we can tell certain things but the universe is different than the one you project it to be.

The linear reality you want to believe in does not exist. Reality is not linear. Your instincts may want it to be linear because

> REALITY IS
> NOT LINEAR

your needs appear to be linear. A nice little linear progression. But Reality isn't that way.

Reality may mean so many things you may not be able to comprehend it at all. You may simply be baffled. Bafflement is good because, when you are baffled, if you ask what's going on, something might slip into your consciousness. Aaah, and this is where humility comes in (again). If you're not humble, it means you have simply decided you are unteachable. You have simply decided that whatever was baffling you "makes no sense." You decide: "Something is wrong. This is stupid. And I'd rather be angry."

But what if you say instead, "Maybe there is something that I don't understand here. Why don't I try to search for an answer? Why don't I try to expand my knowledge of things? Why don't I read something? Why don't I learn something? Why don't I go within myself and try to see? Why don't I talk to somebody?"

At times like those, why don't you become open—because that is what humility would require then. To remain teachable rather than deciding you already know the answer and you already know you don't like it.

So at moments like that, you might want to become open-minded. In fact, very open-minded. And when you do, and you search for an answer, you may find that in this incredible complex universe that is built upon dimension after dimension after dimension, something may come through one of those dimensions to answer your tiny question in your tiny corner of reality that points you in the right direction.

We are Guides and we say "Go this way so that you can find something." And when we do, it is very rarely for the reason you think it is.

THE NATURE OF GUIDANCE

No, we are not trying to play games with you. Whether we come through a medium or through your own consciousness, we are not trying to play games. It is just that this is not a nice and neat little three dimensional world where we could say "go that deep, go that high and go this much over" and you'll be there. Those are the three little dimensions that some people think life is about. But this is not a three dimensional world.

It is instead a complex geometry that not even your most sophisti-

cated or most simple mathematics can help you understand sufficiently. But the guidance we give is guidance that causes you to pen-
etrate the dimensions of time and space—and we don't even have to
say: "Go this deep, this wide, this high."

The answer is a much more profound direction. Answers like:
"Wait." Or: "Stay where you are." Or: "Don't do anything; just don't
move."

You ask us: "Should I do this or that?" And we respond: "Do neither
this nor that. Do this other thing instead." You see? And then you
shout: "What do you mean neither this nor that? Do I do this and
that?" "Well, no," says we. "Well, is it something else?" says you.
"No," says we. "Well, is it something that I am not seeing?" says you.
"Yes," says we. "What is it?" says you. "We can't tell you," says we.
And then you say: "Stop playing these games!"

You see?

Maybe you don't have the context yet. Maybe there are no points of
reference within your known reality. Maybe you must be still enough
to allow some of these points of reference to develop. And maybe
once these points of reference begin to appear—which might seem
tremendously exhilarating and wonderful for you—maybe that is not
all there is either.

That very sort of thing tends to happen when a person thinks they
have become still; then this incredible miracle of coordinated events
and coincidence happens and the person thinks: "This is it! This is
what Spirit wants me to be!" And they go and tell everybody, and it
is so wonderful and everyone gets inspired and encouraged. And then
something opposite happens. Now the person thinks, "Was I deluded? Oh I am so ashamed. And I went and told all those people...."

What happened, really? Were we playing games with you? No. Not at all.

The universe is not linear. Guidance you receive can have a multiplicity of levels and meanings. And you may like none of them. But what if it's the truth? What if part of your pain is because you keep wanting the world to fit the way you think it should be—when that is simply not the way it is. Who are you, anyway, to demand that the universe behave the way you think it should? You must conform to Law. Law does not conform to you.

Do you think one day the Creator will say to you: "All right, you run things."? Aren't you already thinking you are in charge when you think the universe should behave according to your intention, your plan?

YOU ARE NOT IN CHARGE

But you are not in charge. You are not. And if you still believe you are, that is one incredible delusion! You do not run this show. And let me tell you something. You don't want to. Why would you ever want to, anyway? Why?

And I will tell you what causes you, time and time again, to reflexively behave as though you run this show. It is another one of those instinctual demands (and it is not really a bad thing). It is fear: The fear that you are *not* in charge and therefore you are threatened because you believe that you can only be safe if you *are* in charge. Oh what a great delusion that is. Yet your instinct demands it.

But you see there is a higher awareness than that. And it is this: If you had no instinct that said "take control of your destiny," you would not even be a conscious entity. One of the first ways entities become conscious is when they begin to realize that they have a certain amount of influence over their space and their environs. And here on Earth most life forms, plant and animal, try to dominate their environment or work within their environment for their own survival.

So that when you are trying to see if you can run the universe, you are basically doing what every other plant and animal on this earth is trying to do: live more successfully within your environment by gaining a little more control over it. And that takes a lot of effort, continually.

But the most successful species cease seeking to dominate the environment and work collaboratively with it. They seek cooperation, not competition. Those that are in competition with the environment are species which die out relatively quickly. But those that last, that turn out to be most successful, are those that find out how to function adaptively within that environment—in cooperation with it.

So, there is an awareness beyond instinct that is your intuitive awareness—a combination of your feelings and your intellect. Educate your intellect, educate your emotions, and your intuition will grow. It will expand. And you will grow more aware. And as you become more aware, you will realize that you don't have to be in charge of the entire universe. As an old soul, trying to be in charge of the entire universe is the source of your suffering. And somewhere along the way, you may begin to think you are threatened by Life itself. But the opposite is true: You were created so that Life could support you.

A spiritual awakening simply means that you realize this. You realize you are supported by Life. As old souls, you may find that you would like to believe you are supported by Life but you have little trust in it; you have little faith.

That takes us back to the truth of it: You need faith. And anything that builds your faith is something you better get a hold of. Faith is the essential ingredient. You cannot live here without faith. If you don't have it, get it. I don't care how you do it, get it. All of the beliefs in the world are worth nothing without faith. Get faith. Use faith. And trust will come all by itself.

How do you get faith? Seek the spiritual experience and a door shall be opened to you that will guide you through to your faith and through the world.

SIX

CRACKLING ENERGY

What a wonderful collection of souls we have here today. I say "souls" because it is important to understand the true nature of who you are.

What you are is an organism that has been created by your spirit. Your spirit is alive right now and crackling with energy. It doesn't live within your physical body. Your physical body lives within it. And that means that who you are is crackling with energy—right now!

And believe it or not, it is possible—in fact very important—to experience this energy and to take in extra

YOU ARE A FIELD

energy into your field. Allow it to crackle around you and stimulate and physically vitalize your energy. Even as I wave my hands like this, I feel more energy crackling around me. Even if you just think for a moment of what you are truly, your energy will begin to crackle and your auras will begin to brighten. And that is very, very important.

It is important because it leads you to recognize the truth of who you are. And that truth is not a sophisticated intellectual or philosophical understanding. It is a simple experience of being. Just *be* and recognize that you are a field—and that your field extends throughout this entire room, and beyond.

Each one of you has a field that fills up this whole room and each field of yours is at a different density so that you can all exist, filling up this room, without squashing each other. And so you can all feel each other and feel each other's auras. If you simply choose to become aware of it, you can feel each other in your aura.

I can feel you, for example, in my aura. I feel what you feel like—each of you. In fact, if you closed your eyes, you could still envision where everybody is in this room. You can envision it visually. But just as you envision it visually, you could also close your eyes and sense each other's presence, as though there were heat generating from each body, each field. And if you imagined that field extended, you could almost see the shape that each field or aura might be.

We say: You would be "impressed" by that shape. You might think it's your imagination, but actually it's your impression. You might have a sense of the aura's lightness or darkness, its brightness or colors. You might have a sense of emotional impact or a feeling or a presence, subtle as it might be. And if you spent even so much as one minute or two minutes a day letting yourself extend your aura, not only in front of you but in back of you, you would heighten your aura to such an extent that you could, for example, step outside of that door and sense that there was a car about to turn a corner down the road here.

You could do this, with just a little heightening of your energy—even to the point where you could sense who's in the hallway outside, right now. And if we were to become sensitive to who would come into that hallway outside the door, then when somebody did come into that hallway, at least half of you would sense a shift in the energy. And the others, with a little practice, would also sense the shift in the energy. You might not know it's a person, but you would *feel* the shift. You would feel it as though something had been disturbed.

Now extend your attention outwardly into the parking lot, and if I were to ask you how many cars are moving in that parking lot right now, some of you would get it. You would need to test yourselves over and over again in this way to see how that sense works. And if you were to do that, you would develop a trust in that—in that (I'm going to call it) *instinct*.

But many people undermine that instinct by saying, "Ah, this is just a logical deduction; what's the use of this?" But what is logical about guessing how many cars are moving in a parking lot? There's not a single darn logical thing about it! It is just how psychic senses work.

But if you cannot accept it unless you find a reason, and when you can't find a reason, you dismiss it, then that cuts you off from your psychic perception. If you cannot find the logic to support it, then you will not allow yourself to have that perception.

But if you can make up a logic to support your impression, then you'll feel all right about it. And this is exactly how some peo-

> MAKE IT
> MAKE SENSE

ple become very psychic. At first, they don't recognize that they're psychic. They just think they're being logical, and it makes no sense to anybody else, except them. But they say, "Well, it makes sense to me."

So sometimes people who are quite psychic think everybody else is stupid—because nobody else understands their logic! In fact, their so-called "logic" is often totally illogical—but it makes sense to them.

You see? They are not aware that they are responding to psychic perceptions so they make up reasons to believe what they believe. And they think, "Everybody is so silly; they should just figure it out; it's plain; it's obvious for everyone to see!" But it isn't. It's their psychic perception that has allowed them to see it.

Psychic perception borders on the perimeter of what might otherwise seem logical.

Now strangely enough, some people are quite afraid of that. Some people are afraid to stretch beyond what their logical mind might present to them because, when people are on the perimeter of their logical mind, they begin to get in touch with a more chaotic energy.

Besides, when you remain within the realm of your own logic, you can maintain the illusion that you have a certain amount of control over your universe. You think you understand it. And so you feel safe about it. But when you go to the perimeter—and then outside—of your logic, it starts to feel unsafe.

Now to you it may not seem like *logic* that you are going to the perimeter of. To you, it might seem factual. To you, it might seem there are certain facts that are accepted by everyone and therefore they are truth. Like this: "These facts are simply so, and, when objectively looked at, are the same and agreed upon by everybody." But that is *entirely untrue*—because all facts are not things that are so but merely things that vast numbers agree upon. And if something else is found to be so and if authority can prove it, then the *fact*, so-called, changes—and everybody now believes the new thing.

Facts are little more than a collection of common agreements. Reality is not based upon absolutes; it is based simply upon what is agreed upon by the conventions at hand.

When you start to challenge the conventions, it feels unsafe. And those who are very fearful begin to have superstitions about it. This leads to another twist: The most outwardly factual, logical people end up as the most superstitious, even while outwardly denouncing the superstition of others. They would be shocked to be called superstitious themselves; yet their whole mindset is based on fear. That is, they must stay within the realm of their own safe logic because they are superstitious that if they go outside of it something bad will happen to them.

Whereas those who are often accused of being superstitious are often expansive and creative thinkers. They are free and testing

> FACTS VERSUS
> TRUTH

logic all the time and are often the least superstitious and most courageous of people. Why? Because they challenge the conventions. And they are likely the least fearful as well as the least superstitious.

So, it is common that when you begin to get in touch with psychic perceptions, it can bring up whatever fears you have about yourself, your paradigm, and your life. For centuries people have avoided their psychic perceptions because of fear, and have labeled them evil or dark instead. They tell themselves that these are journeys into things that shouldn't be messed around with, shouldn't be played with. Even in this day and age, where you consider yourselves so advanced, there are relatively few who explore their spiritual and psychic perceptions in a totally courageous way.

There are even those of you who separate the whole idea of the psychic from the spiritual. There are those that say, "Oh yes, it's so wonderful to be a spiritual person—but oh that psychic thing, oh, you don't really mess with that! That's that lower stuff." Yes, some of you come from that perspective.

Some of you simply don't think psychic perception even exists. Although it is unlikely that you would be here if you were not at least open to that possibility. And people who come here are not *all that* open to it. Isn't that interesting?

If you're here, you may not believe in anything, but that's different thing than not being open. We don't need your belief and you don't need to believe. In fact, if you believed, how could you be open? You'd already be closed by your belief.

So we don't look for believers. We look for the open—those who often don't believe because they seek to know, not to believe. Those who seek knowledge, who seek knowing, are not believers. They are knowers. They are gnostics. And we welcome gnostics here. Here, we welcome the open, the knowers. As for the believers? Well, we welcome you too if you have come here to know. And if you come to believe here *because you know*, then you're not a believer, are you? You are a knower. You are a gnostic.

SPIRITUAL AND PSYCHIC

The spiritual and the psychic go hand-in-hand. Sooner or later anyone on the spiritual path becomes psychic. Sooner or later, anyone on the path of opening psychically becomes spiritual. They go hand-in-hand.

It is impossible to have one without the other for very long, unless one immerses oneself firmly in the denial of one's own experience. Now this kind of denial is quite possible; many people succeed in it for any number of reasons. For example, there are those that may have locked away deep and hidden dark memories of traumatic emotional and psychological issues from earlier in this life or other lives. And when they begin to open up psychically, it might also reopen some of those lost memories. There is tremendous fear there—and also a tremendous opportunity for healing. But some may avoid that opportunity because it is so frightening.

Yet opening psychically tends to lead to the healing of old wounds from this life and earlier lives. Conversely, early wounds from this life—or from other lives—tend to open a person psychically. You will find, for example, those who have lost memories because of sexual abuse. When they begin to heal, they become very psychic. Because locked away with all those memories and emotional feelings was all their psychic perception. The pain they were in forced them into another dimension. They totally disassociated from this plane, from this dimension, and they happened to get in touch with another dimension. They got very psychic.

Now some get in touch with a more constructive dimension and some get in touch with a destructive dimension. But those who get in touch with a destructive dimension will also have the opportunity to heal. They also have the potential to become quite spiritual as well as quite psychic. And they often do.

Sometimes there are different ways that people are psychic. Some people feel things even though they don't specifically know them. Instead, they experience a sort of non-visual impression in the emotions, usually—either in the form of a kind of open, loving, expansive feeling or in the form of a tight, contractive, closed-off feeling. These tend to serve as a positive or negative warnings. Their intuition tends to work like that.

For each physical sense, there is a psychic sense. We call them the *Clair Sisters*. For sight, there is *clair-voyance*—or seeing

> THE CLAIR
> SISTERS

clearly. For hearing, there is *clair-audience*—or psychic hearing. For smell and taste, there is *clair-gustiance*—walking into a place and feeling: "Something's fishy here." For people who have that kind of psychic sense, it's as though they smell something or they get a bad taste in their mouth.

Taken together, you could call these *clairsentience*. It's an emotional reaction. That's how this type of psychic perception tends to work.

And how do you get psychically more and more clear? Practice. Practice. Practice. Start with small things, things you are not too greatly invested in. When you're trying to get perceptions about things in which you are greatly invested (matters where you care a great deal about the outcome), it's hard to be objective about what is real. Sometimes, until you become more psychically clear, the only things you get an intuition about are things that don't really matter much to you. Caring a great deal about something will color your perception, emotionally.

So practice developing your awareness on things that matter less to you.

One of the best ways to hone psychic ability and get past that particular place is to offer your gifts in service. Have the intention of helping others with your psychic skills more than just focusing on your own life. Get the attention off of you and your investment in the outcome, and then you will begin to see more objectively. In the process of helping others, your own psychic skills will become honed, and you will begin to know things of your own life, more and more. See ways you can serve and you'll get psychically clearer about your own life.

So practice. You'll be wrong sometimes. Part of being "psychic-slash-spiritual" is growing; and one aspect of growing is getting beyond prejudices. Yes, sometimes people project their fears based upon commonly agreed upon conventions of behavior or dress or style; or sometimes people have their own specific way of looking at things.

And yes, some people use their psychic perceptions in a way that isn't worth a damn. Nevertheless, if they are truly growing, those psychic senses will refine. Everyone is going to be wrong some of the time. But if you are willing to extend yourself and be wrong sometimes, you will grow righter and righter.

A few more things. Have any of you ever heard ringing in your ears? And it won't stop? And it confounds you?

Well, that ringing is who you are. It's your soul's resonance. And it often occurs because one is out of harmony with one's own resonance and needs to hear it. By hearing it, you attune psychically and your perceptions become clearer. That is who you are!

Who you are *not* is what's going on in your head. And yet, that is what people most often identify as themselves. And that is why if your thoughts are happy, you may feel like you are happy. And if your thoughts are miserable, you feel like you are miserable. That's what happens when one is identified with one's thoughts.

But when one identifies with who one *really* is—and who one *really* is, is a cosmic resonance—it's a different thing all together. You might say that that ringing in your ears is God beckoning you to pay attention to who you are. That's what the ringing is for!

Now your mind may not be able to comprehend this because what I am referring to here is *Self. God.* And the more your mind tries to figure it out, the more it won't know.

The only thing you can do is *resonate* with it. That's the only way you can figure out what it's for: *Just resonate with it* while you are doing whatever you are doing. When you do that, you may just find that you are not going into some of the same places you have been before that pull you down. Or if you do go into some of those places, you may find that you move through the energy you find there rather than get stuck in it.

So that ringing is a kind of cosmic assistance, an alert signal that we, your Guides and Teachers, are around—because we are tied into your own resonance. And when you become aware of that resonance, you also become aware of us.

LEAVING THE BODY

So maybe you'll hear ringing. Or maybe you'll get goose bumps. Or your hair will stand on end. These are all forms of the same energy, the same vibration, the same resonance. Sometimes it's heard as sound, sometimes it's felt in the body, sometimes it stimulates the chakras—the body's key resonance centers. They are all signs that energy is moving through the body. Crackling. Crackling!

At those times, you are resonating more profoundly—and you need to attune to that. It's a signal for you to remember who you are and to remember the Life-Force that flows through you. Crackling!

You'll get very used to those kinds of things when you've shed your body. There'll be light everywhere and sounds everywhere and all that sort of thing.

And while you still have your body, you'll get a chance to practice what that means when you leave your body from time to time—and certainly every night when you sleep.

Most people go unconscious when they fall asleep; as a result, they are not aware that they leave the body—even though everyone leaves their body in sleep. Everyone! But as you form techniques to become more psychically or spiritually aware, you'll become aware when you leave the body as well. Now, when that happens, you may think that it is the first time you are having an out-of-body experience—even though you have been having an out-of-body experience every night of your whole life. And so that first time can be a bit frightening.

People can become afraid the first time they become aware that they are leaving their body. There are lots of reasons for that. One of the main ones is that they are simply afraid because they don't know if they're going to come back. And if you have any death fears, you are going to find out about them then—if you haven't already found them out.

Maybe you are a person who has heard about a cord—an astral cord—that follows you when you travel out of your body. And maybe you have also heard that you must *never let that cord get cut*. Mataare was worried about that. So I told him, "Mataare, if you're traveling out of your body and you see an astral cord, cut it yourself!" Cut it yourself!, I told him.

First of all, you'll still get back. If you are not supposed to be dead, you won't die. Second, there's no way to cut that cord, anyway. And third: if you're tied to something and cut that tie and come back, you'll come back free! You'll come back unattached. You'll come back awakened. That's why I told Mataare: "If you find a cord, cut it!" You see!

And if you're afraid of dying, then better get over it—because you're going to die.

Sooner or later, it's going to happen and there's nothing to fear about it. There's nothing to fear about death. There really

> YOU ARE
> GOING TO DIE

isn't. The only thing there is to fear is thinking that it might be everything you don't want it to be. *Now that's a fearful thought!* But death is what it is—not everything you want it or don't want it to be.

And there's something else about death. It couldn't be such a bad thing because it doesn't work anyway. Who here believes in past lives? All right! So if you believe in past lives that must mean that you have already died. Right? Yet here you are! So it didn't work, did it? This death thing didn't work! Or you didn't do this death thing very well because here you are!

And that also means, it couldn't be all that bad. Because this, right now, right here, is your afterlife, isn't it? Bet you never knew it would be like this! Hmmm? *This* is your afterlife. You died—and here you are, after. So this is the afterlife.

People also sometimes get afraid when leaving their body because sounds can get very loud. Common sounds . . . the dripping faucet, the ticking clock. Why? Because, again, leaving your body means that your aura is expanding—or, more exactly, that you are expanding into your aura and detaching from your body. When that happens, you become more attuned and more focused and have greatly heightened sensitivity. That sensitivity may make any sound a little bit of a shock.

But the biggest reason why people become afraid when they leave their body, hearing sounds or sometimes seeing things that frighten them, is because the very first plane after the physical plane is the lower astral plane. And that's where you get to meet your monsters, so to speak. All your fears tend to "come alive" there in the lower astral plane. This is exactly where the idea of *Hell* comes from—the lower astral plane.

THE LOWER ASTRAL PLANE

By the way, Hell is not a place where people go to be punished. Hell is not a place to which people get sentenced. But *Hell does exist*. And people do sentence themselves to it—all the time. God does not sentence you to Hell. You put yourselves there because of your own particular set of values and judgments. You put yourself in your own self-created, self-torture chamber, so to speak: the lower astral planes.

Generally speaking, you visit the lower astral planes for two reasons. One, you stop off there, temporarily, on your way to the higher planes. Or, two, if you have any emotions, active or repressed, that haven't been dealt with, you will stop at the lower astral plane in order to have them brought up—and they certainly will be brought up, particularly if you have been in a state of fear or repressed fear.

Especially if you are a spiritual person, you will need to face your fears; so you will likely meet your "dragons" in the astral plane. And, by the way, you *must* meet your dragons. The only way you can graduate from the astral plane is by meeting your monsters, face-to-face. And that's what tends to make people afraid.

You meet your dragons, by the way, not so much to prove yourself worthy, but rather because you need to develop your mastery.

MASTERING THE DIMENSIONS

One does not need to be a so-called *high soul* to get into a high plane. But it is also true that higher souls do not necessarily avoid the lower planes. Otherwise, what would a wonderfully high soul like me be doing in a low place like this? Well, this is not really *such* a low place. This is a place where higher and lower souls both live. And that makes it very very interesting.

Mastery, which is what you're all here on Earth to learn, is being able to go into any dimension, at will, and out of any dimension at will. As part of that mastery, you will learn how to go in and out of the higher and lower dimensions. Even if you are at a so-called *higher level of mastery*, some of your training is in the lower astral plane. And you will have to learn the lesson of the Psalm of David, *Yea though I walk through the Valley of the Shadow of Death, I shall fear no evil.* That is a part of mastery. You must learn to walk and live in the lower astral plane with no fear and that is one of the lessons of higher mastery. So, get used to those lower planes—and part of that is facing your own fears.

By the way, you'll only be taken into the lower astral planes when you're ready—when you've been immersed enough in the higher ones that you're able to embrace the lower ones. That's the most exciting part—the lower plane. The higher planes are not as exciting. Oh, they are very exalted, but all the exciting work is in the lower plane.

Yes, all that exalted experience is very wonderful, but it's here where I love coming because here is where all the work is, you see. Here is where all the Light needs to be. Here is where all the pleasure is for me.

I love a good, dark soul now and then. In fact, quite often. I love conflict. I love what people are afraid of. Those things I have always loved. That is where my passion is. My passion is where darkness is. My passion is to bring the Light. That's my passion. That is my purpose. I love that. There's nothing I could like more than that. Put me in the darkest of all possible realms and let me loose. That is my pleasure.

And being able to go into the highest of the brightest realms. That is also my life, you see.

So that brings me back to this: you are, as entities, wonderfully alive, crackling spiritual and psychic beings. And there is no way to grow in life without also becoming very spiritually and psychically aware. It is, in fact, your destiny. Why? Because you are psychic and you are spiritual. And either you know it and it's opening more, or you don't know it and you're here, finding out that it's going to open very, very soon.

And the reason I went to the trouble of going through all of these descriptions is because you are going to have one or all of the experiences we spoke of just now. That is in your path. There is not anybody here who has not touched upon something we have spoken about. Or everything we have spoken about. Or who will not touch upon everything we have spoken about. We, your Guides and Teachers, say this because that is the only thing that can possibly come out of all of this.

So, prepare to have your psychic awareness open wide. Prepare to see things you didn't see before. Prepare to know things you weren't alert to before. Prepare to heal places you haven't healed before. Prepare to love more deeply than you have ever loved before. Prepare for a few wonderful, unexpected surprises quite soon. Perhaps before even you go to bed tonight. Perhaps before the end of the week. You are about to have a shift in your energy.

Open up those psychic senses and be prepared to recognize when you have sensed something that then turns out to happen.

> OPEN. GIVE
> YOURSELF CREDIT

And make sure to give yourself the credit for it then. "I sensed that," you will say, "I knew that would happen." Just start nodding: "I *knew* that. I didn't know exactly, but I *knew* that. Oh, yes, I know that. I sensed that. I *knew* that. Yes, that's familiar. I don't know why." Begin to acknowledge all your senses. Start saying, "Yes, yes, I understand, I know. I get it. I see. I feel. I had a sense about that." Start turning on those psychic senses and begin to become more and more alive. Your energy is there. Your excitement is there. Your life is there.

Look what it's done to me. I'm so alive I can't stop coming in through Mataare or any other of the other mediums that I come through. I can't help myself. I just keep finding myself here and there. I can't help it. It's a wonderful, wonderful existence. I have so much energy that there are ten thousand Merlins almost, coming through all kinds of mediums in this world. I can't find enough outlets to express myself through.

This energy is also needed as part of my own learning as I embrace new levels. It goes on infinitely. There's no end to it all! One grows forever and ever.

So, that's what I am doing here. I'm very, very glad that I've been brought here today.

SEVEN

✳

PARTING THE VEIL

There is a veil between the dimensions, and everyone has penetrated that veil on more than one occasion. Some of you, in your penetration of that veil, have witnessed something that has caused you to embark upon a search to find out more about what is on the other side of that veil. That which you have touched on the other side of the veil is a spiritual reality—a spiritual reality that, in fact, dwarfs the reality that you experience on the earth plane.

But because your bodies are sensual—designed to experience life primarily through the physical senses, and then to process that information intellectually, emotionally, and physically—there is a tendency for you to focus upon this very small dimension of reality to receive information. And in doing that exclusively, the greatest body of awareness and consciousness is totally and absolutely unrecognized and forgotten.

The body of consciousness is so vast—and human beings at this period in their development have accessed so little of it—that the ways you are living your life from day to day tend to have very little to do with the greater picture. Very little to do with what you were really born to this Earth for. And because human beings take only tiny segments of the time that is possible for learning, work that could be done in perhaps the span of one lifetime takes hundreds of lifetimes instead.

COLLECTIVE CONSCIOUSNESS

There are many things that stand in the way of human beings focusing on what they came here to do. The greatest obstacle that stands in the way of a human being embracing his or her true life's purpose is, you might say, the *collective consciousness*. The collective consciousness (which is made up of the sum total of all the human beings on the planet, and for that matter all of life past) tends to form a body of awareness, or a body of consciousness, itself. It tends to hold its own intuition, its own intellect, and its own primal forces. And all human beings are attached to that collective consciousness.

Now, that collective consciousness has a use. It has a purpose; it is *not* the enemy. That consciousness, being collective, represents a sustaining body of thought that *feeds* all of mankind. At the same time, it also represents the greatest barrier for human beings to get beyond. As human beings begin to access the upper and outer registers of that body of consciousness, they start to feel very alone. There are fewer and fewer people that they are able to relate to. And sometimes those who access this body of consciousness go mad, for they need the support of some kind of collective consciousness to maintain a frame of reference. If there is no frame of reference, there is a feeling of being lost, alone, empty, abandoned, frightened, and overwhelmed. It is maddening. And I speak from experience.

As I grew up, I grew more and more impatient with many of the human beings around me. Actually, I couldn't stand human beings; and so I went off for great periods of time into the woods to live by myself—to discover life and existence.

When I was 160 years old, I decided I wanted to get married. I didn't look old; and I decided that I didn't want to take a wife who, so to speak, was my own age. I didn't even want a woman half my age! I didn't want to marry an 80-year-old woman. I wanted a young woman. Puberty, in my mind, was not too young. I mean that's what old men often do, don't they, marry the very young?

Truth be told, I was in love. Her name was Gwendolyn, and she was very very young. So I married her.

I claimed Gwendolyn. And then I left her to go off into the woods by myself. I left for almost a decade. I never sent word. I simply left. And when I came back, I discovered that Gwendolyn was living with a man. But she was my wife! And even though she hadn't heard from me in nearly ten years, I still expected her, so to speak, to act the part.

I killed the man. It's called murder. And he, by the way, was a friend of mine.

Yet I felt fully justified, based on my culture and my time. Mind you, at that time, I was what some of you might call "an advanced and learned soul." And a very spiritual one! Yes indeed! So advanced that I married a very young woman, left her, came back many years later, killed her husband (or, more accurately, her lover—who had been more of a husband to her than I had ever been). And then I left again and never thought twice about any of it.

All of it meant very little to me at that time. Very little. I simply expected that Gwendolyn would behave in accordance with the way I thought she should behave. And I fully expected that she should have understood that I was about more important business.

Now you must understand how it was in those days. We didn't have police officers. We didn't have courts. We didn't have judges. We didn't sit around pleasantly in rooms with carpets on them, in nice heated or air-conditioned places, with lights you could switch off and on.

Back then, whatever you had, you had to hold on to if you wanted to keep it. Even if you didn't want to keep something, you had better act like you did. Because if you did not act like you wanted to keep what you had (even if it wasn't all that important to you), then you were a nothing. And being a nothing could be dangerous for your survival. So there were certain statements of property that had to be made.

And this situation with Gwendolyn was one of them. I did her the wonderful favor of marrying her; then disappeared into the woods and never saw her again for a very long time. Then I had the audacity, when she was with someone else after years of my not returning, to come back and kill the man. Then I went back off into the woods again. Delusion!!

Now do you know why I'm telling you all of this? Hmmm?

Well, I wonder how much you feel you are right, how much you feel the things you do are justifiable? I wonder how much you think is due you and what you think is supposed to happen and how things are supposed to be. And then when that is not the way it happens, I wonder how much of what you feel is right and wrong is simply based upon your being a product of your environment and your culture? I wonder.

And how much do you really know about what is right and wrong, ultimately? How much do you know about how things are supposed to be?

Now I'm not saying this to challenge you; I'm just saying that I thought I knew—and I found I didn't. I used to think that the more I knew, the more control I would have over my existence. And the more control I had, then the more I could justify the particular set of affairs that I lived amongst.

Well it wasn't about that. It wasn't about that at all. Not for me.

I've learned a great deal, but one of the greatest things that I've learned is that I know very little. That's one of the greatest

> KNOWING LESS
> IS FREEDOM

things that I've learned. The more that I've learned, the more I became smart enough to know that I actually had learned very little.

The more I knew, the less I knew about. I've become smart enough to know that I don't know *anything*. And *that* has freed me so incredibly. It has freed me to be happy! Because, you see, I used to think I *had* to know these things. I used to think that the more I learned, the more I knew.

Now, I am not suggesting that you don't learn. I am suggesting just the opposite: *Learn everything you can so you can find out that you don't know anything.* Then you can be free! You see?

I'll take a few questions.

Question: What's the difference between bliss and ecstasy?

Merlin: From a very young age, I was a mystic. Somewhere in my journeys, I came across a young avatar who was in the state of *nirvikalpa samadhi.* He was laughing all the time; he was terribly infectious. And I loved it!

He disappeared from my life soon after I met him, but I recognized his state to be of great reality, of great value. And I sought it. But what

I found by seeking bliss—meaning a state of happiness and no other state—was madness, not ascendancy. Madness! Now I don't know whether that young avatar was mad or not, but I knew that bliss wasn't for me.

It's sort of like this: Where did I get off thinking that one state held all the lessons? And that's the same lesson that I was having here in this world.

I realized that no matter how good or bad a thing is, if it remains the same, it's a trap. It's a prison. I realized that you have to be able to move on in order to grow, not stay in the same place. And I learned this not only about the world but also about bliss. I learned that about any single state of being and about any single place.

<table>
<tr><td>GOING INTO
THE LIGHT</td></tr>
</table>

For example, some people imagine that an afterlife is like a heaven and that "going into the Light" means "going to heaven." Well, I have news for you (and you don't have to believe me), the time will come when your relations will urge you into the Light or you will enter the Light through your meditation—and strangely enough in both cases, you can then find yourselves *back here*! How did that happen? What the hell are you doing back here?

Well, it's because the Light said "Enough!" and kicked you out and said, "Get about the work." You see? You are no use to the Infinite there, doing nothing in the Light. As long as there are dimensions of creation and existence in which there are un-enlightened beings and not-yet enlightened beings, something must reach out to those who have not crossed the border.

Now all of you have been in the Light before. People go into the Light to become harmonized with It. It is as though you are in the

Light and getting a "download", as you call it. Once that download is complete, you must go and download it somewhere else, so to speak. If you don't go and do that download, you feel as though you are missing the point.

Now all of this is missed if you have a very self-centered existence. If what you are here for is *my* security, *my* growth,

MY—ME—ME—MINE

my needs, *my* love, *my* realization, *my* understanding, *my* truth, *my* this, *my* that, *my* realization. Self-realization. Self-acknowledgement. Self-belief. Self this! Self that! You are one very self-centered being.

It doesn't matter how spiritual you think you are. Such a self-centered being cannot get very far. They can get *alone*—that's what they can get. You are not here for that.

Yes, you need a certain amount of those things. But sooner or later, by the time you are an older soul, you will find that all of your consciousness—all of your situations, circumstances, and challenges—must be resolved on a plane of spirituality and a plane of altruism. All your answers must—and will—come from there.

It is a long journey, but there is no one who sits in this room who is not well advanced in all that.

Let me put it another way. Everyone sitting in this room is an old soul. I am speaking to you. And the truth is: You already know! You have arrived. Each of you has arrived at that point where you feel less than complete when you don't feel useful to others. Each of you has arrived at that point. Each of you does not like to feel separated from your fellows. Each of you is in joy when your fellows are able to *receive from you* in some way. You are here as an expression of the Light. You are old souls!

That's the long answer to your very short question about the difference between bliss and ecstasy. Bliss is one very beautiful state. But there are other states of being that become rich as one awakens as, no doubt, you have experienced in many dimensions of your life. Haven't you? You already know that there are many states of emotional fulfillment that are not necessarily happiness or bliss or any singular state.

TOO MUCH POSITIVE

It's sort of like this. There is positive energy and negative energy. Some people have made a mistake in thinking that positive is good and negative is bad—when, in fact, there is good positive and bad positive as well as good negative and bad negative. Good-and-bad and positive-and-negative are not the same thing.

Too much positive is not good. Try it and find out for yourself. Too much negative is not good. If you haven't found that out, try that too. No negative is bad! No positive is bad! You need good positive and good negative experience. And you need good positive and good negative energy. You cannot focus on the positive entirely because you will find: *It isn't good*!

Are there any other questions here? Yes?

Question: You talk about focus on self and focus on Source. Are those the only two conditions? Or are there any other conditions to focus on?

Merlin: Ohhhh yes! Yes! But they cannot all be articulated. What I have expressed here is extraordinarily simplistic. There are a number of other dimensions of reality that are valid and valuable to each of you on your personal path. And all those truths, metaphysics, and understandings are a gift to you from your Creator about which you have something to learn—and about which you have something to teach.

However, the essence of it all, the fundamental truth behind it all, is that there is a self—and that is you—and there is that which is greater than yourself—and that is God. It's as simple as that. And, the twain *must* meet.

And when they meet—when self meets that which is greater than self—that is where the delicious journey begins. But if self knows nothing greater than itself, it is painful and it is fearful. And the other side of that is: If that which is greater than yourself does not know you, It is sad, and It hurts. The Infinite cannot stand the separation anymore than you can.

The Infinite may not be a personified being, as some people like to create it. But it is also not an objectified being, as some others would have it be. The Creator is a potent expression. The closest description that contains what the Creator is (and it doesn't really contain it) is *Love*—Love that is unconditional and unlimited.

At that level, it isn't like a love that you call love, except to the extent that you have realized this Creator-Love—because at that level, Love is

> LOVE IS
> POWER

equal to Life. It is equal to the Life Force. It is love on the purest level. That which contacts God reflects aliveness of some kind. Another way to say this is joy. That does not mean there is never any sadness. But what you can be certain of is that wherever you see joy, there is the unmistakable presence of God. Even if that joy comes and goes, there is the presence of God because that is the aliveness that is a part of that being.

So Love at the purest level does not resemble affection although affection can easily come from it.

Love at the purest level does not resemble kindness, either, necessarily—not as you define kindness. But *tremendous* kindness comes from it! Love is the source of many expressions of beauty, including those things. And Love is the source of many expressions of emotion. But Love itself is not an emotion. Love is a *power*. And it gives birth to many emotions.

What do I mean by the *self*? All your ideas, conscious and unconscious, of who you are. And that self is a pretty mighty thing. It is very expansive. But it isn't infinite. And when the self comes into the presence of the Infinite, not only do you have growth but you have a psychic shift. You are no longer who you were. You have contacted a power greater than the self, and you keep transmuting by that contact, by that contact with the Infinite.

And yes, you contact many other points of focus that are useful for many things, usually, for example, some form of healing that is necessary for you to learn so you can pass it on to others who are sick and suffering.

You know of course that it helps to meet people where they need to be met—because not everyone can be met at the same place. By your own God-contact, you become an entity that becomes aware of how to meet other beings where they need to be met.

You develop particular talents and skills related to this, whether as healers, helpers, fighters, doers, creators, doctors—yes, even attorneys—and artists, musicians, and so forth. People find their service and help people connect from where they are to where they need to be to go to the Source.

So yes, there are many, many points of contact and points of focus. And you have had many of them already. But for you, as an old soul, the Source is the Infinite. And you must bring yourself to the Infinite and say: "What would you have of me? What would you have of me?"

And most of the time, the Infinite will reply, "Wait. Wait. I hear you. Wait." Now the wait is never very long. Sometimes, you think it's very long because you're really looking for something else, some specific answer. And then a little later, something happens like the last person you wanted to hear from calls you up on the phone—and the Creator says, "Now!"

And perhaps you miss that "Now!" and say instead, "Dammit! I asked to be of use and then *this* happens!" You missed

TRY IT! TRY IT!

it. And then you go into your meditation that night and ask, "Creator, what would You have of me? I can't find anything. What about this that I'm working on, Creator? What about that?" And maybe you hear nothing. But really, it's "Wait. Wait. Wait."

Then something else you don't expect comes around the corner. It's not always bad things, you know, or difficult things. People tend to recognize the good things that come along—something very sweet happens or something very nice or some strange, peculiar synchronistic event. And you shout: "Yes! I knew! It finally came. I prayed! I sought! I asked! And here it is! A sign came before me!"

And you get very excited about it; and you run with it—for a while. And then, inevitably, you come to a place where it

WAIT. WAIT. WAIT.

all seems to run out of steam. But that's not because it's over. It's because things are going through a few permutations you didn't expect. So you go in again and ask, and usually the message is: "Wait. Wait."

After a while, what used to take a focus to try to understand becomes an organic part of your intuition. Then you're not hearing or feeling "wait" anymore. Instead, you find yourself stumbling more and more into circumstances that work because your attitude is receptive, your mind is open, and your heart (having been made humble) puts you in the right places at the right time. And all this becomes a working part of your intuition. That's how it tends to work.

Let me ask: Who here has never felt as though they have been assisted? That is, has everyone here felt at some point that there must be something—but you just can't always get in touch with it? Sometimes you see signs of it. Sometimes you're not certain. Has anyone here never had a time where they felt that there was some sort of Presence in their life, even though it didn't do what they wanted it to do? Is there anyone here that has never felt that? Who's completely blank, has no idea, who says, "Nothing like that ever happens to me. I'm so out of it! No matter how hard I try, it's useless!" Is there anybody here that has that experience?

GRADUAL AWAKENING	But has everyone here had that experience sometimes? Yes? Yes! That's part of the gradual awakening.

If you happen to be like the Buddha, the brother many of you are jealous of, then you might not have had moments where you lost it. But for the rest, you are getting it—you are getting it in flashes. But it's the moments when you're not getting it that trouble you, isn't it.

I am here to say that this is how it works. It comes gradually, in flashes. And there is a reason for that. If any of you don't know that reason, then the ones who do know that reason can explain it to you. And the ones who do know that reason, know that when they have been on an accelerated path that, for some reason, is too accelerated, they have felt a pain which they realized and said, "I want things to slow down."

Has anyone ever been there? Yes! So when you see the wonderful newcomers to their enlightenment—souls who are just beginning to wake up and are full of enthusiasm and vim and vigor, who just want to run on that path—you want to tell them:

> No, no, believe me. You don't want to end up giving up your job and leaving everything and throwing everything away. You don't want to do this. Believe me. Be careful because you don't know where it's going to take you. You don't know."

And they say, "Oh no. Look what just happened to me. I'm just going to do it!" Many of you have tried to accelerate your path, and it has been enormously uplifting—at first. At first! Then some time later you found yourself in a hole. Haven't you? That doesn't mean it's wrong. But you have found yourself there, nonetheless.

And some of you have heard a lot about the techniques and methodologies of awakening and mystics who are able to travel into other dimensions, float in the air, and manifest things from nothing. And you say you want to learn those techniques too. "How do I learn that and where?" You want to accelerate your path.

Well, Sun Bear, a Native American who often comes through Mataare, talks about one of the ways he did it—one of the ways he accel-

GETTING INTO
A HOLE

erated his path. He got into a hole, naked, for five days—it's a common Indian tradition. No clothes. Nothing but a blanket. No food. No water. Just get into a six-foot deep hole, five-foot wide, and sit there. And wait for God.

By the third day, you're pretty close. By the fifth day, you're talking to the birds, the ants. You understand the whole universe. You are in the other dimension. You have the messages. The vision comes.

Now, it's not likely that many people know the power of a thing like that and will do something like that, or have done something like that. It is much more likely that one day you'll wake up with an inspiration, after pleading with your Creator: "I just need a change."

And your Creator says something like: "Go to the Southwest." That's how you got there. "It's time. It's time now," you say, "I must do it! I don't know why. I just have to do it!" And then there you are, sitting in New Mexico, asking yourself, "Now, why did I come here? Here I am in bloody Albuquerque. What am I doing here?"

That's your hole! You see! You didn't get into a hole, naked, for five days. In-a-hole-naked-for-five-days-with-no-food-or-water is just too tortuous. You went through it for a year and a half in Albuquerque because you would much rather take the year and a half of torture to see God than that little five-days-in-the-hole-naked-with-no-food-or-water route.

What is the purpose of that? What is the purpose of either? I will tell you: to get outside of the paradigm in which you have created your safety. To get a view of beyond.

FACING THE
DARK SIDE

But you must cultivate the faith, the love, and the trust first *before* you do that! Because you will face the dark side. You will face every fear. You *must* face the dark side in order to enter the Light. You must! Either by exhaustion, by depression, by choice, or by spirituality, you must face the dark side. You must have the dark night of the soul—several times, usually. And if you are wise, you will cultivate a connection with the Infinite first—in order to have it to hold on to as you go through that dark night. And when you do, you will be given the serenity to be able to meet whatever calamity you must meet.

You must face it. You must face the shadow. That's the way to the

Light. You can't purify yourself of the dark side. The dark side will walk right with you, but you will no longer have fear of it. And the dark side will remind you.

Now that doesn't always externalize as demons and trouble. But that dark side is as necessary as a shadow when you walk in the face of the sun. You cannot eradicate your shadow. And you'd better not try to fight your shadow—because the shadow will win. There is nothing you can do to get rid of it.

But it's harmless. It's not bothering you. Don't make an issue of the shadow. If you're there boxing your shadow, that probably means your back is to the Light. So face the Light and let your shadow stay behind you. That's the lesson of Yeshuwa in the desert when he said: "Get thee behind me, Satan." You've heard of that, yes?

Yeshuwa said: "Get thee behind me, Satan!" Very smart. Turned his back. By the way, that wasn't Satan; but it was close enough. (I was there. I was a spiritual guide once upon a time to Yeshuwa. He returned the favor.) So if you are boxing with shadows, you are not facing the Light. You *must* face the Light! And when you do, the shadow will be behind you. Try to get rid of that shadow and you're in trouble.

So the time comes when you go through the dark side when there is literally no Light that can cast a shadow. All there is is darkness, all

A WORKING FAITH

around. That's when you will need your experience, your faith. Faith! That which you have gained as a result of having spiritual experience, in the past. That's when you remember that experience. You have learned from it. You have experienced it before. Faith is not a belief. It is a trust, based upon experience.

And you must have a working faith. Sometimes people have faith until something happens; they don't have a working faith. You must have a working faith.

So that's why things happen *gradually*—so you can develop experience and work from that experience, carry that experience to meet your difficulties, utilizing the faith and the trust you have gained from having had that experience. And you let that experience be tested until there isn't any fear of the darkness anymore. And that happens gradually.

Otherwise, what would you do if you were put in the pit in order to shine as a light before that? And you will be in the pit, sooner or later because the Light always sends the enlightened to where there is darkness. Think about it! What good is all that Light going to do where there is already light? The Light must go where there is darkness in order to carry the message—in order to carry the Light.

So you are going to find yourself first facing your own shadow, and then also facing shadows that are externalized to you. And what you are there for will be revealed.

Yes, existence is a beautiful thing and what good is it if you are nowhere? It's wonderful to be *somewhere*. I like to be somewhere so much that I'm always several places at once. I simply can't get enough of being somewhere.

So I'm very happy that my journey has brought me exactly *here*. Gathered together here with you, journeyers through the dimensions, at this single point, in this wonderful mystical experience.

If you could suddenly see and *remember* every place you've ever been throughout all your incarnations and remember every particle of your awareness, you would still find this moment very, very special.

In fact, I would go so far as to say that you would find nearly *every* moment very special because you would know how every moment is a tremendous convergence of synchronistic events. One can hardly believe such a thing is possible. And yet it is!

And I also say this: "If there were a language which the Creator could speak and it were something that human beings were also aware of, the closest language would be mathematics." And the reason I would say the closest language to the Creator would be mathematical is because it would take a sophisticated understanding of mathematics to appreciate how powerful this moment is—this tremendous convergence of synchronistic events.

SYNCHRONICITY

If you could comprehend the synchronicity of this particular moment, you would be *mathematically astounded*! Why, I would wager that you would fall instantly flat on your face in prostration before the Creator. I am certain of that. Because you would see how impossible such a moment like this really is. It is such a clever arrangement!

This never ceases to amaze me. And my amazement has been extraordinary in ways that you could never possibly imagine—and not always pleasant. And I don't mean only since I've been here in this world. I mean since I've been here in this world *and* since I've been here in the Spirit world. I remain amazed. In fact, I have never found a point at which I could *not* be amazed. And that is amazing! I simply cannot believe the simplicity of it all, this tremendous convergence of synchronistic events.

The things I've learned just from coming through Mataare, for example, have been so powerful to me—and so beautiful.

We are not islands, you know. None of us are, though I tried to be.

The dimension where we (the Guides) dwell is where you live too—right now, with us! We are here amongst you and you are amongst us. It's not that we live in some dimension up there and you live in some dimension down here. We are *all* here. And there's a certain amount you need to be aware of us, and a certain amount we need to be aware

of you. But we don't need to be aware of you too much, and you don't need to be aware of us all that much.

| GUIDES ARE HERE, |
| RIGHT NOW |

We live amongst each other. Even though some of you may have met me for the first time in this way, we know each other in a far more important way than that *because* we dwell together in some other dimension *where we are one*.

And when I say *where we are one*, I do not mean that we all blend together and become one common expression. We are like an orchestra that makes a common music—even though there are separate instruments. We are together in that sense. There is a place where we are all together, and we know each other in that place.

And that place need not be veiled to you. When your emotions go up or down, when your life flows better or worse, those conditions do not separate the place where we are one. All that is required for you to know this is a little love, a little simplicity, and a little seeking. We are beckoning you to come and join us. And all you need to say, if you wish to, is: *Yes*.

And say it often! "Yes! I want to be consciously a part of that dimension of Love and Light. That's what I want!" And then "it" starts to get much better.

And I will tell you something else: It is not bliss everyday. First of all, there isn't a "day." But it isn't bliss all the time. Oh no, no, no, no. It isn't bliss. *It is ecstasy!* And I cannot tell you the sweetness of the pains that I have felt, as well as the joys that I have felt. I have known nothing like this kind of sweetness.

So I urge you to continue on your journey, and create and deepen your contact with the Infinite, and seek its Source for your guidance. And the veil between the dimensions shall disappear. It doesn't happen *in* a day. It happens *every* day!

ACKNOWLEDGMENTS

By now you know that this book was 14 years in the making. A long time.

I couldn't get it to become. I couldn't get it to be a book. It just sat there in chapters for years. I sometimes suspected that those delays, which were legion in number and length, were more due to Mataare's humility—a certain reluctance on his part to embrace the enormity of his gift and be seen. And so the first thank you that I so willingly give is to Mataare.

Truth be told, I do not know Mataare all that well. In fact, we have probably spoken a total of five hours across the past 14 years. He is a private person. And he is also not around much during the channeled sessions. He says hello, a few of-the-moment comments, the prayer of protection, and then he's gone. When he comes back, he says hello—usually with a bit of surprise that there are so many people staring at him. Then it's good night and the room empties.

Because Mataare heard the call, because he listened, because he was willing to put up with unimaginable intrusions into his personal life, he has my greatest thanks, my unwavering admiration, and my love. Mataare, you cannot know the depth of my gratitude that you are simply on the planet and ready to serve through your gift. Many join me in those thanks from the depth of their hearts.

In these 14 years, so many have given support, love, encouragement—and the work of their fingers to this project. So many typed and transcribed all those darn tapes: and to all I say: "Thank you so much."

Grace Burneka is first amongst these. Grace worked in a key position in my company for a number of years. She was eager to transcribe tapes from the very beginning. In fact, she *was* the beginning. And as she transcribed, I do believe she became a fan of Merlin. Sara Kane, already Merlin's student, also transcribed for hours, making her way through acupuncture school; she touched this book with her beautiful energy in that way and more. Camilla England gave to the book as well. She is probably the fastest typist I have ever met, even though her real gift is in writing words, not transcribing them.

Diana Asay spent years with me and those tapes. How many Saturdays did we sit together mulling over the tapes in an attempt to catalogue them? Diana, a gifted teacher and wizard in her own right, spent months sorting through candidate sessions, doing rough and fine editing. Diana, you gave so generously of your time, your mind, and your heart, at a time when I thought this book would never happen. My thanks to Mary Junewick, as well, for her brave attempt to move this project off the dime.

Dawn Bothie, herself a gifted channel of Merlin and other Divine entities, was and is a sister of compassion to me. Always encouraging me in my vision, Dawn (and often enough her Merlin) was a voice of comfort and peace during a very bumpy ride.

Rania James, a superb astrologer and sublime musician of voice and piano, was unflagging in her support of any and every Mataare book I ever talked about. She too had been smitten.

Aurelia Navarro, my constant partner in books, proved once again that she hears and supports the author's unique voice—in this case, Merlin's. In many ways, I have found compiling and editing someone else's words to be far more challenging than writing my own books. When I write for myself, I simply listen. But when I worked on this book, I had to hear. Somehow those are two different skills. If we have had success in that, I lay my thanks at Aurelia's feet. She kept me from several sins of both omission and commission as far as Merlin's voice was concerned—stilling my impulse to simply delete certain tricky passages and allowing others to stand that needed no help. A point of balance and wisdom and an exceptional editor, Aurelia has proven her gifts once again. And I am thankful.

And in a companion breath, I thank Bill Stanton. What did he contribute and to what scale? You have it in your hands—the beautiful page layout of this book and its exquisite cover. This is the intuitive genius of a master designer. Bill, if you go into the Maine woods, please do not go far. There are more books we must do together. Many more. Your designs will capture the essence of them. Your covers will draw people near.

My love and appreciation go to Wally Chapman, as well, who keeps saying *yes* to sudden demands on his talent. Thank you, Wally, for your careful reading and your intuitive understanding of the importance of this book.

Thank you to those many who gave the gift of love as money to this book: Jacqueline and Robert Miessen, Robert Zubic, Annette Mason, Jan Caviness, Odette Suter, Alyea Sandovar, Fabienne Suter, Clifflyn Bromling, Gayle Grimes, Kenneth Kafka, Kathy Bennett, Caryn Young and an additional Anonymous donor. As much as any of us, you helped make it happen.

And finally, I thank the master teachers and Guides who are in and of my Life. First and ever, Swami Chetanananda, Guru of my Heart. And with the same heart: Rudi, Phylos, Sun Bear, Davorra, Enoch, Jenerick Toraneck, Fubi Quantz, Paramahansa Yogananda, Jahweh, Yeshuwa, Miriam, Metatron, Azlo, and, of course, my ancient-in-years-only partner, Ambrosias, the Merlin.

Thank you for giving me this opportunity to bring your beauty further into this world. I am honored. And I am renewed.

Gwendolyn

✦

About The Medium

Mataare lives in Florida with his wife and two children.

www.Mataare.com

✦

INDEX